Management in
Further
Education

Theory and Practice

Dedication

To Andreas, Alexander and Naomi

Management in Further Education
Theory and Practice

Harriet Harper

David Fulton Publishers
London

David Fulton Publishers Ltd
2 Barbon Close, London WC1N 3JX

First published in Great Britain by David Fulton Publishers 1997

Note: The right of Harriet Harper to be identified as the author of this work has been asserted by her in accordance with the Copyright, Designs and Patents Act 1988.

British Library Cataloguing in Publication Data

A catalogue record for this book is available from the British Library

ISBN 1-85346-473-2

Typeset by Textype Typesetters, Cambridge
Printed in Great Britain by the Cromwell Press Ltd, Melksham

Contents

Acknowledgements

I would like to acknowledge all those people in FE colleges with whom I have worked and studied for many years. These students, lecturers, managers and support staff have unwittingly contributed to my thinking. I am particularly grateful to Andreas Credé for his guidance and support and also to Sandra Lawrence for so willingly sharing ideas. Thanks are due to Diane Brace for her advice and constructive criticism and to Charles Atkinson for suggestions. I am also grateful to those who provided assistance, material, examples or ideas and in particular: John Mowbray, Barry Lewis, Adrian Perry, Bernard O'Connell, Walter Bruce, Marie Dooley, Beulah Coombs, Gavin Dykes, Hazel Brookman and Juliette Birchall.

Examples used in this book are based on real situations and people. They have been provided by the author herself or by colleagues from a variety of colleges. In most cases, however, names and titles have been changed to retain anonymity.

Harriet Harper
London
January 1997

Introduction,

WHY DO FE MANAGERS NEED THEIR OWN MANAGEMENT BOOK?

Being a manager in a college is, in most respects, no different from being a manager is any other organisation. The fundamental requirement for the job remains the same: to manage people, tasks and information, to allocate scarce resources, and to ensure the continual monitoring of services or products.

There are literally hundreds of books and articles on management and the contents of some of these will be discussed throughout the book. The vast majority, however, relate specifically to large, well-known corporate companies. Many are based on research undertaken in the USA. Of those relating to service providers, few are aimed specifically at education. Those that are tend to focus on schools and universities.

This book is not an alternative, it is a starting point. It attempts to introduce key management theories and ideas and to contextualise them specifically for the FE audience. It also provides pointers for those who wish to pursue further management research in more depth. Throughout the book, examples and quotations are provided to illustrate the theory as it applies to FE.

The book includes chapters on people, operations, resources and information. This division is convenient for the structure of the book but, clearly, management is complex and all these topics are interrelated. People and information, for example, could be included in one chapter on resources. Some themes, theories or writers, therefore, are referenced in more than one chapter.

Management skills and knowledge have assumed greater importance since the 1992 Further and Higher Education Act, which instigated a shift to a market model of FE, with colleges operating in a competitive environment. Consequently, a major culture shift is taking place in colleges, despite a traditional reluctance to embrace industrial or commercial methodologies.

In terms of its size, achievements and impact, FE is an impressive sector. England's 450 colleges provide education and training for more than three million learners. They enrol more full-time students aged 16–18 than all schools, including independent schools. In addition, there are significantly more adults studying in colleges than there are in universities. In terms of 'efficiency', colleges have achieved substantial productivity gains: unit costs were reduced by 11% in the period under local management (1989–1993) and by a further 20% since incorporation (1993–1996)[1]. While there are understandably concerns about retaining an acceptable level of quality, it should be noted that, typically, inspectors report that approximately 90% of lessons observed in colleges are satisfactory or better, compared with 80% in secondary schools and 70% in primary schools (ACM 96)[2].

In many towns in the UK, colleges are among the major employers and are often owners of extensive land and premises.

WHAT CAN FE MANAGERS LEARN FROM GENERAL MANAGEMENT THEORIES?

Management theories are not about providing the right answer or the 'correct' way to manage a team, section or college. Most research, on which theories are based, does not result in dramatically new findings. Management research tends to examine current thinking and produce a little more evidence which may or may not support existing theories. This, in turn, leads people to develop new theories.

A college section leader, studying on a management course, recently said to her tutor 'Just tell me how to manage my team'. If it was that easy all organisations would be expertly managed. There is no management toolbox. The toolbox idea is, of course, appealing – it implies that management consists of a series of tricks that anyone can perform after practice. But a tool cannot replace thinking. Management is not about fixing things; it is about creating the conditions in which people are able to accomplish their professional objectives effectively.

Most management theories are inductive. This means that conclusions have been drawn from observing managers at work or interviewing them. As such, these theories cannot be proved right or wrong. There are also books based on the views of successful chief executives, outlining their philosophies and how they manage their own highly successful organisations. They are there to use and to learn from but that does not mean that they are necessarily appropriate for your circumstances, in your college. Their value, however, lies in the fact that they draw conclusions which attempt to explain behaviour or actions, and they can be relevant to the work of a wide range of managers. As a manager in FE, this can be useful in a number of different ways.

It may provide you with a new vocabulary enabling you to understand and explain behaviour and actions in your college. Theories allow you to generalise and they may confirm your 'gut' feeling about certain aspects of organisational behaviour. Learning about the research others have undertaken encourages reflection. It may inspire you to be proactive with a greater degree of confidence. As well as helping you to understand your own management style and that of others, it may motivate you to experiment with the strategies that you use. You have the option, of course, to reject other people's findings. In doing so you are likely to adapt what you learn to your own situation and develop your own models.

The next section provides a background to developments in management thinking, focusing on key movements, ideas and writers, many of which are revisited in future chapters.

DEVELOPMENTS IN MANAGEMENT THINKING

Theories about the best way to manage organisations have developed and changed over the years, reflecting, to a certain extent, the prevailing attitudes of the time. The past thirty years, in particular, have seen a variety of themes and 'fads', as well as a whole new vocabulary of management. A brief background to these ideas will provide some insight as to how and why organisations are run as they are today.

Scientific management

The scientific movement which arose during the first two decades of the twentieth century has had a lasting impact on organisational practice.

Its chief exponent was F W Taylor (1856–1915), whose name has become synonymous with scientific management. 'Taylorism' is associated with the division of work into its smallest, simplest elements; mass production and assembly line industries. Taylor[3] outlined how his methods could increase the efficiency of production, lower costs, increase profits and enable workers to increase their productivity. Through scientific methods of job analysis, he believed it was possible to establish the best and most efficient way of working. 'Every single subject, large and small, becomes the question for scientific investigation, for reduction to law'[4]. Workers needed to be trained in these efficient production methods and given jobs they were best suited to do. Taylorism was extensively applied by Henry Ford in his Detroit car factory. This in turn provided the model for mass production techniques subsequently adopted worldwide.

The scientific approach saw people as rational, economic beings, motivated by money. Taylor believed that workers, if paid a fair piece-rate, would increase their productivity in order to maximise their earnings.

Other proponents of scientific management included Frank and Lillian Gilbreth[5] and also Henry Gantt[6] (mostly associated now with the type of bar chart he developed to demonstrate how far a task had been achieved in relation to the optimum target).

The classical approach

Classical management is a collective term for a set of ideas which were propounded by individuals from different backgrounds and countries, primarily between 1920 and 1950. The approach was concerned with general principles of management, which could be applied to *all* organisations, regardless of the type of institution concerned. Classical theorists have been credited with having brought a formal and rational approach to management for the first time.

While Taylor focused on the shop floor worker, Henri Fayol (1841–1925) began at the top of the hierarchy. Like Taylor, he believed that a manager's work could be reviewed objectively and analysed. His principles of management and his ideas as to what constitutes the tasks of a manager are well known and often referred to. Many management courses still begin with identifying his five functions of management, as illustrated in Figure 1.

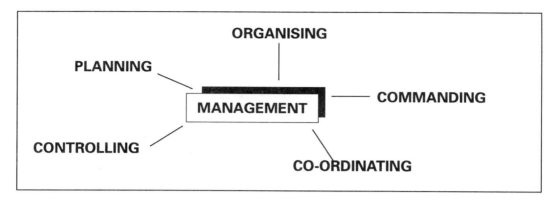

Figure 1 Fayol's five functions of management, developed in his *General and Industrial Administration* (1916; translated C Storrs, 1949, Pitman)

The human relations approach

This approach is concerned less with organisational structure and more with people – their needs, motivation and behaviour. The most influential writer was Elton Mayo (1880–1949), who studied working conditions at the Hawthorne plant of the Western Electric Company in Chicago between 1927 and 1932. The Hawthorne studies demonstrated that people could become motivated by being consulted about decisions affecting their work and by being part of a social group.

The Hawthorne studies are discussed more fully in Chapter 1 on Managing People, as are the other main proponents of this human relations approach to management: Maslow, McGregor and Herzberg.

The systems approach

The systems approach takes the view that an organisation is a collection of interrelated and interacting parts. A college, for example, is an open system. This means that, as well as containing a number of sub-systems, it also interacts with external environments. It receives inputs from a range of sources and it also provides outputs, as illustrated in Figure 2. The soft systems approach, documented and used by Peter Checkland[7] amongst others, provides a structured methodology for resolving complex organisational problems. Drawing boundaries around the problem issue to be resolved, managers and others involved can consider all the elements which impact on this issue and recognise the influence of related systems and of the external environment.

The contingency approach

Contingency theorists argue that approaches to management should be adapted to meet the specific needs of an organisation and that these needs change. Unlike others, they do not claim that there is *one* way of managing and that the same principles can be applied to *all* organisations. Different management problems

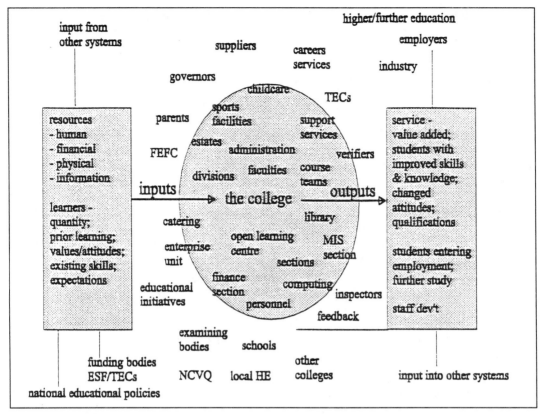

Figure 2 FE as a system

require different solutions and what is best for one institution may not be appropriate for another.

Key writers and ideas of recent decades

The past decades have seen management theory in a state of flux. In examining the main changes that have taken place mostly in commercial concerns, it is possible to identify how they have also been reflected in the FE sector (some years later, in many cases). It is not suggested that colleges should mimic private sector companies. However, much can be learned from a critical examination of what has been happening in 'outside' institutions. Colleges, like many other corporations, have attempted to transform themselves from sprawling organisations with elaborate hierarchies to leaner, fitter institutions, confronting the same issues of quality, customer care and competition.

Each decade is discussed below, focusing on key writers, ideas and themes.

The sixties – size, strength and strategy

Back in the sixties the received wisdom was that size was might and management was about power and control. Companies were large, safe, slow-moving organisations where you could climb the career ladder and where jobs were for life. Poor performance resulted not in redundancies but in dispatch to a backwater to serve out time. Many would argue that some colleges remained like this up until the eighties.

Much management debate, at that time, revolved around the importance of sound strategy. A key publication was *Corporate Strategy* by Igor Ansoff[8], who remains influential in this sphere and who continued to write on the subject into the seventies and eighties.

The seventies – cultures and complexity

Although strategy was identified to be a key factor in terms of success, research undertaken by Henry Mintzberg (1973)[9] revealed that managers were not, in fact, reading and talking about strategy. Mintzberg provided insight into how managers *actually* managed – rushing from crisis to crisis, firefighting, preferring action to thought and basing decisions on hearsay rather than factual information. Far from being reflective, systematic planners, 'managers work at an unrelenting pace . . . their activities are characterised by brevity, variety and discontinuity, and . . . they are strongly oriented to action and dislike reflective activities'[10]. His research on chief executives also found that, rather than using aggregated information from a formal management information system, they strongly preferred oral communication either by telephone or face-to-face. Moreover, the vast majority of these oral contacts were arranged ad hoc.

The complexity of organisations was recognised by Mintzberg, Rosemary Stewart[11] and Charles Handy. Handy's *Understanding Organisations*[12] examined the workings of organisations in detail and paved the way for his many popular books in the eighties and nineties. It was recognised that if different organisational cultures existed they had to be managed accordingly. The theme of cultures is explored more fully in Chapter 2.

The eighties – quality, excellence and change

In the early eighties, quality came to be seen as the key to success in organisations. The American W Edwards Deming, already well known in Japan, was finally discovered in the West. He and Joseph Juran spread the quality gospel and sparked interest in the 'Japanese' approach to management. Japanese management techniques were studied and became a rich source of ideas. Quality, of course, remains an important issue for FE and is discussed in Chapter 2.

'Excellence' also emerged as a key theme, with the publication of Tom Peters and Robert Waterman's book *In Search of Excellence*[13]. Peters and Waterman had worked as consultants for the top management consultancy firm McKinsey in the United States. Passionate and positive, the book described what was already being done by 'excellent' corporations, without necessarily imitating the Japanese. Excellence was based, to a large extent, on being customer-focused. This led people to believe that their organisations could become more successful if they adopted the behaviour, structures and actions of the companies described in this book.

The 'you can learn from how I did it' theme continued with a spate of popular books written by successful chief executives, such as Iacocca of Chrysler[14] and Akio Morita of Sony.[15]

Less populist but more logical and analytical was Michael Porter's framework[16] for understanding how companies create and sustain competitive advantage. He went on to propose[17] another framework called the 'value chain', a systematic theory of examining all the activities an organisation performs and how they are linked to one another.

Change and turbulence were recognised as features which were here to stay. Books and articles attempting to analyse change and identify ways of managing it became increasingly popular. Most notable were Rosabeth Moss Kanter's *Change Masters*[18] and Tom Peters' *Thriving on Chaos*.[19] The management of change is discussed more fully in Chapter 2.

Colleges, too, were experiencing transformations in the eighties, particularly in relation to new curriculum initiatives and changing local education authority cultures. However, the most significant change, in the form of incorporation, was yet to come in the early nineties. While many argue that the Further and Higher Education Act of 1992 was radical, others suggest that the market orientation of the FE sector came about gradually, starting in the eighties, with a series of reforms brought about by government legislation and an increasing inclination within the sector to provide a responsive service.[20]

The nineties – empowerment, re-engineering and learning

With the recession of the late eighties and early nineties, organisations began to flatten hierarchies, 'downsize' and talk of empowering employees. Managers were learning how to coach and listen, rather than control and direct. With the rapid advances in IT capabilities, the widespread use of personal computers and the recognition of the strategic importance of knowledge and information, employees became known as 'knowledge workers'. Many prominent writers, such as Peter Drucker[21], Alvin Toffler[22], James Quinn[23] and Robert Reich[24] heralded the arrival of the 'knowledge society' in which knowledge is the most important resource in society.

Organisations focused on their 'core competencies', retaining their key employees and outsourcing all other activities. This resulted in dramatic changes to employment practices. Many more people were – and still are – working on fixed or short term contracts providing these outsourced services and many have several such jobs on the go at once (a 'portfolio' of work, to use Handy's term). Compulsory redundancies occurred for the first time in colleges.

Business processing re-engineering (BPR) has provided the nineties with its major new idea. With BPR, if something is not working, you identify the process and start over again from scratch, re-inventing *what* you do and *how* you do it. A re-engineering case study, from FE, is discussed in Chapter 4. The key work to influence this development was an article by Michael Hammer.[25]

Those writing about 'the learning organisation', such as Peter Senge[26], argue that in a climate of uncertainty and technical transformation successful organisations will be those who can learn, adapt and innovate.

Survival depends not just on technological innovation in a narrow sense but on wide-ranging creativity that enables organisations to thrive in a difficult world.

Organisations are having to adapt to external changes much more often and much faster than in the past. This means that employees have to be able to learn and to continue learning.

CONCLUSION

FE has adapted the language of the private sector, including mission statements, human resource management, total quality and empowerment, all of which are discussed in future chapters, illustrated by real examples. It is critical, however, to think about the context in which managers work when trying to apply any theories and ideas. Highly successful management strategies used in a Japanese car factory, for example, may not be appropriate for use in FE. Colleges are neither factories nor 'businesses' in the traditional sense but managers in FE are now working in a more 'businesslike' environment. The drive for improved organisational performance is as unending in FE as it is in most other sectors. An understanding of the development of management thinking by reflective practitioners should therefore prove to be invaluable.

REFERENCES AND NOTES

[1] Association for College Management (1996) *Funding Further Education into the 21ˢᵗ Century – A Submission to the Public Expenditure Survey on behalf of Further Education Colleges.*

[2] *ibid.*

[3] Taylor, F W (1911) *Principles of Scientific Management* Harper and Brothers.

[4] *ibid.*

[5] Gilbreth, F B and Gilbreth, L (1916) *Fatigue Study* Sturgis and Walton.

[6] Gantt, H (1919) *Organising for Work* Harcourt, Brace & Hove.

[7] Checkland, Peter (1981) *Systems Thinking, Systems Practice* John Wiley.

[8] Ansoff, Igor (1965) *Corporate Strategy* Penguin.

[9] Mintzberg, H (1973) *The Nature of Managerial Work* Harper and Row.

[10] *ibid.*

[11] Stewart, R (1985) *The Reality of Organisations – a guide for managers* Macmillan.

[12] Handy, C (1976) *Understanding Organisations* Penguin Books Ltd.

[13] Peters, T and Waterman, R (1982) *In Search of Excellence* Harper and Row.

[14] Iacocca, L (1986) *Iacocca* Bantam.

[15] Morita, A (1986) *Made in Japan* Fontana.

[16] Porter, M (1980) *Competitive Strategy* The Free Press.

[17] Porter, M (1985) *Competitive Advantage* The Free Press.

[18] Kanter, R M (1983) *Change Masters: Corporate Entrepreneurs at Work* George Allen and Unwin.

[19] Peters, T (1987) *Thriving on Chaos* Macmillan.

[20] Elliott, G (1996) 'Educational Management and the Crisis of Reform in Further Education' *Journal of Vocational Education and Training* Vol 48, Number 1.

[21] Drucker, P (1993) *Post Capitalist Society* Butterworth Heinemann.

[22] Toffler, A (1990) *Powershift: Knowledge, Wealth and Violence at the Edge of the 21st Century* Bantam Books.

[23] Quinn, J (1992) *Intelligent Enterprise: A Knowledge and Service Based Paradigm for Industry* The Free Press.

[24] Reich, R (1991) *The Work of Nations* Alfred Knopf.

[25] Hammer, M (1990) 'Reengineering work: don't automate, obliterate' *Harvard Business Review* July–August, Number 4.

[26] Senge, P (1990) *The Fifth Discipline: The Art and Practice of Learning Organisations* Doubleday Currency.

CHAPTER 1

Managing People

INTRODUCTION

Flexibility for academic, support and management staff has become a feature of FE, as in other sectors. While taking on a whole range of new and changing roles themselves, managers are expected to coach others, who in turn are adapting to the requirement to be multi-skilled. The introduction of human resource management strategies, as opposed to what is traditionally recognised as the 'softer' personnel role, has emerged in FE as a result of a number of factors: the introduction of the College Employers Forum (CEF) contract for lecturers; quality assurance arrangements and performance indicators; Training and Development Lead Body (TDLB) assessor and verifier awards, inspection and appraisal. Managing people in this type of environment is complex. This chapter discusses the issues involved under three themes: individuals, teams and self.

INDIVIDUALS

In this section, the concept of empowerment is discussed, followed by a review of the theory and practice relating to motivation. The contributions of key theorists, such as Mayo, Maslow, Herzberg and McGregor, are examined in relation to their implications for FE managers. Issues relating to the management of disagreements, poor performance, uncooperative staff and complaints are addressed and the section concludes with a discussion of appraisal in FE.

Empowerment

Many organisations proudly proclaim that 'people are our greatest asset'. In FE, it is clear that the quality of staff really does make a critical difference. With all the uncertainties associated with the recent changes in organisational structures, funding and curriculum developments, the ability to motivate staff is a matter of high priority for managers in FE.

Much of the recent and current theory relating to human resource management and motivation centres around the notion of 'empowering' individuals. Empowerment is about giving people control over their working lives. It heralds a departure from older, more traditional methods of command and control, which characterise hierarchical organisations. In an empowered organisation, layers of supervision are removed and the role of the manager becomes one of support, coach and provider of direction and resources. In many cases in FE, management layers have been removed due to external financial pressures, rather than an explicit desire to re-structure in such a way as to empower those lower down the hierarchy.

Empowerment means giving power to make decisions but the problem remains of deciding *which* decisions should be taken by employees. If decisions are held too close to the top, employees will not be fulfilling their responsibilities and exercising their authority. On the other hand, if too many decisions are pushed too far down the organisation, there is the risk of lack of coherence and conflict in different parts of the whole. Employees cannot be truly empowered unless they have the discretion to take whatever decisions they think at the time are appropriate for them to take. There is clearly a risk. The people empowered are more exposed and their managers are less in control.

How does an empowered workforce provide a better quality service? In a college, where value is delivered primarily through personal interaction and group work, the human element is of paramount importance to the delivery of a high quality service. In this kind of environment, people need to be giving one hundred per cent effort in the right direction all the time. It can be argued that a purely top-down management model is less likely to provide the necessary flexibility and motivation.

Many employees feel better about their work if they know that they have more control over it. Individuals' high morale, if widely shared, can also give an organisation a positive quality that is often visible to outsiders, such as students, parents, governors, employers and inspectors. It is then reciprocated by them, resulting in a feedback loop of positive feeling.

This, in turn, can improve customer service. If lecturers or support staff in contact with current or potential students are able to make decisions themselves and provide an appropriate response, they will also give the impression, quite correctly, that the student is dealing with people who know what they are doing.

When employees know responsibility for outcomes rests with them, they are likely to take action swiftly and locally to solve problems. If they do not need to raise operational issues up the hierarchy, they can make the appropriate horizontal connections themselves. Cross-functional teams can form and re-form as necessary without the agreement of senior or middle management.

Improved performance, high morale, speed of action, superior customer service and flexibility are recognised advantages of an empowered workforce. Another important issue for the future may be compensation for limited career paths. Increasingly, there are fewer promotion opportunities in colleges. As with many organisations, colleges will need to find other ways of motivating and rewarding people. Broadening their responsibility and authority – with support and training and without overloading them – is one way to accomplish this and to provide challenging and rewarding employment.

There are, of course, difficulties in establishing the right balance when attempting to empower people within an organisation. Half-hearted attempts can result in chaos. One employee, for example, may be willing to go further than a colleague in taking care of a particular need, leaving students or employers with different levels of service. Departments may evolve different policies on everything from register design to verification procedures. Usually these conflicts can be resolved by policy statements but this, of course, weakens the distribution of authority. The flexibility and speed that result from distributed decision-making can lead to a lack of clarity about who is responsible for what.

Although improved morale is often cited as an important advantage of empowerment, it should be noted that there will be those who do not want the responsibility that comes with this style of management. Lecturers may well argue that they just want to teach – they do not want to be burdened with involvement in other decision-making processes.

Empowerment is not about removing layers of management and simply expecting those left to pick up the work, without any support or training. There is no point asking people to take on responsibilities unless they have the information to judge what should be done and the power to achieve the required results. It is not about simply abdicating responsibilities.

Example

'I hold regular team meetings with my site childcare managers. I noticed that one of them, Nasriya, was becoming particularly awkward and negative recently in these meetings. I talked to her after one of the sessions to try and find out what the problem was. It seemed that she was less able to cope with the demands than the other two. She didn't want to take the operational decisions without checking with me and she felt she needed much more advice and information. She was less experienced in her role than the others and felt threatened by their confidence.' *The Director of Support Services*

Reflection

This director had recognised the need to delegate for her own sake. She also consciously wished to 'empower' her team to provide them with greater job satisfaction. However, she failed to recognise that different people need different levels of support and direction. While two of the childcare managers were pleased with their new roles, Nasriya was floundering and was reluctant to admit it.

There is an argument that empowerment actually reinforces hierarchical control if people receive power from their superiors, rather than because it is logically and intrinsically built into their jobs. Mintzberg supports this view[1] and uses the analogy of the beehive. The queen bee does not empower worker bees. She has no role in the genuinely strategic decisions of the hive, such as the one to move to a new location. The bees decide collectively and the queen simply follows. The queen is responsible, however, for what has been called the 'spirit of the hive'.

Motivation

The issues of empowerment, job satisfaction, trust and expectations feature in many of the main theories of motivation. These ideas are described and discussed below, commencing with the Hawthorne Studies.

The Hawthorne Studies (1927–1932)

Elton Mayo is often referred to as the founder of the human relations movement.

His research put to rest the totally mechanistic approach of scientific management, which assumed that people were motivated by material considerations alone. His work highlighted the importance of groups in affecting the behaviour of individuals at work and enabled him to make certain deductions about what managers ought to do. At the Hawthorne works of the Western Electric Company in Chicago, two groups of workers had been isolated, to explore the links between fatigue and working conditions, and lighting for one had been varied and for the other held constant. No significant differences in output were found; whatever was done with the lighting, production increased in both groups. This led to the view that paying attention, showing interest and discussing work with people results in improved performance.

Example

'People in the department were really anxious about the impending FEFC inspection. All the preparations and trial runs made it worse. The inspector observed sixteen lessons in the three days he was with us. To my amazement, once he had gone, several lecturers expressed disappointment because they had *not* been observed.' *Programme Area Leader*

Reflection

People had worked hard, preparing good lessons with appropriate documentation. They wanted their contribution to be noticed and to be recognised and to feel involved in the whole inspection process.

Mayo went on to undertake a series of experiments between 1927 and 1932. They were amongst the most extensive social science research projects ever conducted. Thousands of workers were observed and interviewed. The aim was to increase productivity for the company. An unexpected outcome, however, was that the studies revolutionised social science thinking.

Taken as a whole, the significance of the Hawthorne investigations was in 'discovering' the informal organisation, which is widely accepted today. As a result of his research, he concluded that

- an individual's attitude to work was shaped strongly by the group to which that individual belonged within the organisation
- the informal group was able to motivate an individual at work
- effective communication between manager and subordinates was critical to achieving improved performance
- people were motivated by more than just pay and conditions
- the need for recognition and a sense of belonging was important
- improvements in working conditions alone provided only a short term improvement in performance

Example

'I went to find Glen, one of our new lecturers, to give him a message. I expected him to be with the GNVQ foundation Business group. There was no one there. It emerged that although students were down on the timetable for two hour sessions, they were, in effect, only getting about 40 minutes "contact" time. The students were arriving up to thirty minutes late (and tutors were waiting until they were all there before starting the lesson). They were then given a break in the "two hour" lesson and again they arrived back from the break at different times. When I tackled Glen about this, he said that all the other tutors did the same.' *New Head of Department*

Reflection

A powerful group norm had been established. Tutors in this section were, in effect, in collusion with each other and with the students. Glen had been anxious when he started the job to tackle the problem of late arrivals and so discussed this with the course leader. The course leader dissuaded him from any action, presenting the argument that there was nothing that could be done about it. Glen reluctantly accepted this and had slipped into this group behaviour. The Head of Department needed to address *all* the team and not just Glen.

Maslow's hierarchy of needs

Probably the most well known theory of motivation is Maslow's hierarchy of needs. Maslow argued[2] that all humans have the same basic needs and that we move progressively up a hierarchy, as shown in Figure 3. Firstly, we need to survive, e.g. we need food and water, and then we need security, e.g. somewhere to live. From there we seek company and the feeling of belonging. Once we have all these needs satisfied we need prestige and finally we look for self-fulfilment.

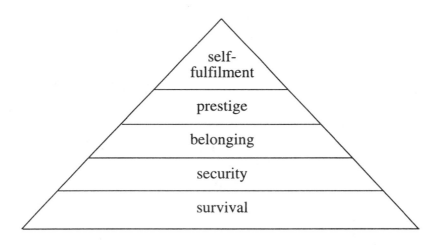

Figure 3 Maslow's hierarchy of needs

Maslow believed that a satisfied need is not a motivator. Once you are well fed and safe, for example, you stop being preoccupied with food and shelter. He also believed that a need is not effective as a motivator until those lower down in the hierarchy are satisfied. Artistic or scientific challenges, for example, do not motivate you if you are still struggling for food and shelter.

It is not a direct journey and some people go up and down the hierarchy at different stages in their life. One criticism of this theory is that it has an American bias and, as such, does not take into account the characteristics of other cultures where achievement is not necessarily a major life goal.

However, this theory may help to understand people's behaviour. It may be possible to identify those colleagues who are clearly seeking prestige (e.g. promotion) or self-fulfilment (e.g. studying part-time). One could also argue that in these uncertain times many more FE lecturers and managers have actually moved *down* the hierarchy and are now concerned about the lower levels of survival and security.

Example

'Gill came into FE from industry. She seemed very dynamic and, although not teacher trained, everyone felt she would make an excellent teacher. However, she never really enjoyed the job and left within two years. When discussing with her the reasons for her departure, it was clear that, although she did not have serious disagreements with any of her colleagues, she never felt "one of the group." ' *Director of Studies*

Reflection

While Gill had passed the survival and security stages, she needed the feeling of belonging. On a practical issue, she was in a staff room with people from another section and it was a long walk to where the rest of her team were based. Although not the only reason, this physical isolation contributed to the psychological isolation she felt. Her manager recognised – too late – that he should have given her much more support, particularly as she was new to FE. He failed to provide a mentor, even though it was College policy to do so, on the basis that none of his team had the time.

Herzberg's two factor theory

Herzberg (1968) undertook research with engineers and accountants and found that there tend to be two factors that influence job satisfaction. Firstly, *hygiene* factors, which cause dissatisfaction, such as inadequate pay, unpleasant working conditions and poor working relations with colleagues. These factors are extrinsic in that they are not directly related to the job itself.

The second factor is related to *motivators* or *satisfiers*, which improve job satisfaction, such as a sense of achievement on completing work; recognition from others; responsibility and 'growth' and varied and interesting work. These factors are intrinsic in that they relate to the job itself.

Herzberg concluded that an improvement in hygiene factors does not improve job satisfaction – it merely decreases dissatisfaction. Subsequent research has confirmed this theory and found it to be appropriate in many circumstances.

It is useful to consider what your colleagues dislike about their jobs. When asked to identify problems in her appraisal interview, a lecturer may tell you that she

- has too much administration to do
- does not have her own computer
- works in a crowded staff room
- has a dreadful timetable with no breaks on a Wednesday.

As a manager you may be able to deal with these issues. It is important to recognise, though, that if you remove some of these hygiene factors you will succeed in reducing her dissatisfaction but that does not mean that she will be more motivated. To increase motivation, you need to identify the satisfiers. Asked what she considers to be her main achievement last year, she may say that it was the fact that almost all her students did well in their coursework. This is a clear example of a motivator in that it provided a sense of achievement. When asked what she would like to teach next year, she may say that she would like to be involved in a new curriculum submission or to teach an adult class.

If, as a manager, you can provide motivators, you are more likely to increase that person's job satisfaction and performance. While it is rarely possible to ensure that all lecturers teach only the classes they like, managers can still provide motivators in the form of recognition and feedback. Positive reinforcement, such as congratulating people, acknowledging and praising good work when appropriate, is recognised to be a very powerful motivational tool indeed.

Example

'Sam came into my room in an almost hysterical state at about five to nine one morning. When I asked him what the matter was, he told me that the photocopier was not working. He then went on to say how typical this was of the whole college and then he moaned about almost everything and everyone. As a result, he was late for his class.'
Head of Department

Reflection

Clearly, mending the photocopier would not improve Sam's motivation. People do not work harder once the photocopier is repaired. They just stop complaining about it. The photocopier, in this case, was the 'last straw' and had provided an opportunity for Sam to express his anger. His manager, though busy herself, recognised that he was very stressed and took the opportunity to arrange a meeting with him later that morning. The problems were not all resolved but the outburst over a seemingly unimportant 'hygiene' factor shed light on a whole range of other issues, including his dissatisfaction at having to teach numeracy to the Leisure and Tourism group.

Theory X and Theory Y

Douglas McGregor (1906–1964) and his Theory X and Theory Y[3] is often discussed in terms of describing leadership styles. The theory is also used, however, as a framework for considering the motivation of employees.

If line managers subscribe to Theory X they assume that people dislike work and must be coerced; are reluctant to assume responsibility; are happier with clearly defined tasks and are resistant to change.

A Theory Y manager, on the other hand, believes that individuals will usually work hard without coercion; they can exercise self direction and control; they seek rather than avoid responsibility and they possess potential for creative work. McGregor concluded that people are more motivated if they work for Theory Y managers. In choosing between the two approaches managers make assumptions about people's motivation and treat them accordingly.

In thinking about yourself or other managers in your college, you may recognise X and Y types. One could argue that in FE people have traditionally been given considerable responsibility and freedom and that most managers naturally tend towards Theory Y. It may be helpful to think of changes that have taken place in your College since incorporation and whether or not this has resulted in a move towards Theory X.

Example

Overhead in college canteen. 'Tony (the IT technician) was saying how annoyed he was that no one told him about the planned changes to the IT Centre. He said that the worst part was that he had some good ideas. No one bothered to tell him about the changes, let alone ask him for his views.' *Faculty Administrative Manager*

Reflection

The manager responsible had taken a Theory X approach and assumed that Tony would not be interested in contributing. This was a missed opportunity to get Tony on board; to involve him in the changes and to listen to his views. Tony may be less motivated now as he feels no ownership of the decisions being made.

Expectancy theory

Expectancy theory asserts that people are motivated by their expectations that certain modes of behaviour will lead to desired events. In order to be motivated you have to have both the *desire* for the outcome and the *expectancy* that you can obtain the goal. If people believe that a particular behaviour will lead to a particular outcome but place no value on that outcome, they will not be motivated. Similarly, if they place a high value on a goal but expect the probability of getting it is zero, then again they will not be motivated.

Example

There was a promotion coming up in the School of General Studies. The Head of School was looking for someone to lead the development of a new curriculum initiative. He implied to staff that this role could help someone to gain the type of experience needed for the new job. In discussing the promotion, Paul said 'No thanks. I'm not interested in all that hard work and, anyway, I don't want the promotion. It's not worth it for all the work you have to do'. Elaine was heard to have said 'I'm quite interested in leading the course. It might look good on the CV. However, I don't stand a chance of getting the promotion, so I won't bother.'

Reflection

Neither Paul nor Elaine were motivated to work harder because of this impending promotion. Paul did not value the outcome and Elaine did not expect to succeed. The post went to an external candidate.

Disagreements

Managing disagreements with people is one of the most unpopular aspects of a manager's role. In the majority of cases, problems are resolved without the need for formal action. If a disagreement does lead to invoking formal disciplinary procedures, it can involve time-consuming and emotionally draining legal complexities. Even if it does not progress to that stage, it can still hurt. Future working relations may be at stake and potentially even a person's job. The manager's judgement and credibility can also be open to question.

Conflict is often symptomatic of weak management. Ideally managers work to anticipate and prevent conflict and to deal with disagreements before they erupt out of control. Poor handling of disputes can divert effort and energy from where they are most needed and undermine morale.

Non-formal 'every day' disagreements can be managed using one or more of the strategic styles identified by Kindler.[4] Which one – or which blend of two – you use depends on the situation and the people concerned. Each style is described below, with an example.

Maintenance Avoid confronting differences or delay making changes: 'I take your point but the course has already started. It doesn't make sense to implement changes now. Let's give ourselves a breathing space and leave it until the next course.'

Smoothing Accentuate similarities and play down differences: 'Go ahead with the meeting without me. I've got another appointment. You know my views – I'd rather we put the work through the Enterprise Unit but I'm open to suggestions. I'll leave it to you to decide.'

Domination Induce, persuade, force compliance or resist: 'Until we have set up the new base room, I want you to use the annexe. I appreciate it is not ideal but it is only temporary.'

Decision rule Jointly set objective rules that determine how differences will be handled: 'We need people from our section to be on duty for the advice session next Thursday evening. I suggest that those of you who (a) were not able to attend open day last week, or (b) did not get asked to cover for Lorraine's absence, or (c) are not teaching on Thursday evenings, put yourself down on the rota for one hour each. Is that OK?'

Co-existence Jointly establish a basis for both parties to maintain their differences: 'OK. As an interim measure, let's agree to using the old tutorial documentation on your course with the full-timers and the new material with the part-time students. We will then evaluate both at the end of the term and aim to implement the most successful on both courses.'

Bargaining Jointly seek means to split differences, set trade-offs or take turns: 'I'll give up the two rooms in the south-block, if you give us back the large room on the third floor of the north block.'

Non-resistance Offer no resistance to other person's views, blending their efforts with yours: 'I don't think changing the break times will have any effect but I'm not going to argue. Go ahead and we'll see how it works out.'

Supportive release Release the issue, stipulate any limits and provide support: 'I don't think that the hours are appropriately apportioned in the submission document but I recognise that you have discussed it with the team and that you all think it is a sensible solution. I'll support you when it comes to the validation.'

Collaboration Jointly problem solve to integrate views: 'We've only recruited five so far on to this course. It's not viable to offer it with so few students. What action should we take? Run with it for a week and hope that more will enrol? Merge them with another group? Advise them to take a different option? Any ideas?'

Poor performance

Dealing with poor performance in relation to lecturing staff is fraught with difficulties. Strictly speaking, selection procedures should eliminate incompetent applicants. This, of course, does not always work. To address these problems, more and more colleges now require applicants for lecturing posts to give a presentation or to prepare a lesson plan in advance of the interview. A candidate who has obtained a professional teaching qualification is basically a competent teacher but there remain other issues to examine and discuss, for example, the extent to which their experience and skills match the specification. With newly appointed managers, many assumptions are made about the transferability of skills. Assessing people's potential, as distinct from their ability to undertake a job as it currently exists, is particularly difficult. Once in post, it is more difficult to address the issue of poor performance.

Poor performance may be due to a lack of training, inadequate supervision or too much pressure. Often, ill health or pressure and poor performance continue in a reinforcing cycle. Problems with teaching staff usually come to light initially through complaints from their students. With improved quality procedures, greater 'customer focus' and students' charters, these complaints are assuming a greater importance and they require action to be taken. (Dealing with complaints is discussed below.)

Formal appraisal systems and focused staff development programmes should help to avoid problems escalating.

It is not the intention here to delve into the legal aspects of disciplinary procedures. Colleges have their own systems and managers will need to familiarise themselves with the procedures and documentation as well as the legal context when faced with a dispute, if not before.

Example

'Although there were clear policies and procedures for dealing with staff disciplinary matters, I favoured the informal, relaxed approach. This meant that when students or colleagues made a complaint, I pulled in the "accused" and had a cosy chat aimed at appealing to reason and to their better nature. In several cases it worked. However, in the case where it failed it was a disaster. Having not followed college procedures and having no written evidence of what had taken place I was unable to move to the next level of disciplinary action. At best, this delayed action. At worst, it meant that students had left college before any visible effect had resulted from their complaint.' *Head of Engineering*

Reflection

It is critically important to document any relevant incident and to recognise the value of using college procedures. These procedures provide protection for all parties and set the issues in perspective.

In an attempt to appear approachable and friendly, managers may be reluctant to tackle marginal or poor performance. They may feel that it is inappropriate to question the conduct of a fellow 'professional'. As well as procrastinating about the aspects of the job they do not like, managers may fear hostility from the people concerned and from other colleagues. Although possibly legally defensible, resorting to disciplinary action will appear to be very heavy handed.

Actively managing, rather than avoiding, poor performance can enforce standards and thereby reduce feelings of injustice. People rely on managers to maintain order in the work environment and to control those who do not 'pull their weight'. There is an argument[5] that fair and properly administered sanctions actually enhance employee commitment.

Example

'All the other lecturers in her team were complaining about Emma. They were all men and I felt that they may feel threatened by her working in a traditionally male section. Although irritated by her behaviour, I kept defending her as each reason for absence seemed plausible – ill health, poorly relatives, accidents, childcare problems, tenancy disputes, to name just a few. I didn't document them as individually they seemed insignificant. Only when looked at cumulatively later on in the year did I appreciate just how many lessons she had missed and that she had failed to mark assignments and set exam papers. She continued to abuse the system until we had to take formal disciplinary action. I realise that I allowed misplaced empathy and sensitivity to get in the way of sound professional judgement.' *Section Head – Computing and Electronics*

Reflection

Poor performance must be tackled for the benefit of all parties, but particularly for the students concerned. The issues need to be addressed objectively, sustained by facts. Other people in the section understandably felt angered by the fact that she 'got away with it' for so long and that this behaviour appeared to be unofficially sanctioned by the Section Head.

Uncooperative people

Uncooperative people are usually aware that attitudes are intangible and that it is therefore extremely difficult to apply sanctions. They tend to stop short of open defiance. The motivation strategies discussed earlier may not be successful with this type of uncooperative person. However, it is worth attempting to make people feel valued, drawing on their strengths and talents and involving them in new initiatives or some aspect of decision making. Sometimes a negative attitude is so ingrained that the individual has lost sight of how it is perceived by others. Putting the person on the defensive by challenging views expressed or asking for proposed solutions can have positive results. It may, however, be appropriate to assert authority from the outset and explain that certain types of attitude are unacceptable.

Example

'David was incredibly negative about everything. He'd been like that for as long as I can remember. In meetings, he would sigh, "tut", avoid eye contact and slump into his chair. He would teach up to his contracted hours but would avoid contributing to the work of the School in other ways. Any idea was dismissed as "rubbish". In the classroom, he was an effective teacher but he disliked everything to do with the "management" of the School. As a course leader, he refused to recognise that he, too, was a manager. In the past we had all just ignored his outbursts or comments. However, we tried a new approach. We started challenging his views and we took on board a few of his suggestions. He hasn't changed overnight but he is becoming a little more human.' *Head of School of Construction Technology*

Reflection

Ignoring David's attitude was, in effect, condoning his behaviour. Confronting him and demonstrating that the School can value his input may start to pay off.

If arranging an interview with a member of your team to discuss a complaint, an unacceptable attitude, specific incident or poor performance, the steps outlined can act as a useful guide:

- seek the advice of the personnel/legal section beforehand and familiarise yourself with the formal procedures, even if you think it is just an informal meeting
- have all the relevant documentation available and read it again just before the meeting
- explain the purpose of the meeting and how you aim to proceed
- talk about facts you are aware of and refrain from making personal attacks
- be specific and explain exactly what the problem is
- provide evidence to support your concerns and do not refer to any

unsubstantiated rumours
- listen actively to the person's response and take notes, if appropriate
- allow silences to give the person time to think and reflect
- keep the discussion to the point
- probe, if appropriate, to gain more background to relevant issues
- summarise what you think the person has said
- provide an opportunity for the other person to suggest improvements, if appropriate
- obtain a commitment to improvement, if appropriate
- arrange a follow up session to assess progress
- confirm the interview in writing, with a clear summary of the discussion and agreed targets with dates.

Customers' complaints

The charter culture and recent political and economic factors have led to an emphasis on users of public sector organisations as active consumers rather than passive recipients of a service.

According to one survey[6] almost one in six colleges in the UK has been threatened with legal action by students and almost one in four said that students had cited the Students' Charter in official complaints. It could be very costly, therefore, for a college in terms of financial penalties and damage to its reputation, to take its responsibilities lightly.

Although managers may find dealing with complaints frustrating and not particularly satisfying, the process can be useful. Complaints provide a useful source of information about how the organisation is catering for the needs of its customers. In some cases, investigations resulting from complaints unearth undiscovered problems.

As with any of the other companies discussed above, prompt informal responses can often resolve the problem. If left unattended or not seen to be taken seriously, complainants become increasingly frustrated and, as a result, are more likely to invoke formal procedures. Dealing well with complaints, on the other hand, can in fact engender more loyalty than was present before the negative experience.

Example

'A mature, partially sighted student complained to me that one of the lecturers had made an inappropriate remark about his disability, which he felt was not in line with our equal opportunities policy or with the Students' Charter. I acted swiftly, calling in the lecturer concerned. He confirmed that he had made the remark but felt it was a funny "quip" and that it was not offensive. I asked him to try and put himself in the student's shoes. There was a lengthy debate about equal opportunities. He agreed to apologise to the student that day. I documented this meeting and sent a copy to the lecturer concerned. I also advised the student of the complaints procedure in case he wished to pursue it. The student accepted the apology and did not take the matter further.' *Head of School*

Reflection

It was important for the manager to recognise this as a serious issue and to take a lead in implementing the equal opportunities policy by demonstrating her own commitment. She dealt with it as a matter of urgency and the prompt and effective handling of the situation satisfied the student.

It is important to try to balance the needs of the customer with equitable treatment of staff. Managers also have to ensure that performance continues to be satisfactory (or improves) whilst maintaining good working relationships. Even if the complaint is clearly unfounded, the subject of a complaint may polarise the issues, insist that others take sides and feel demoralised by the fact that the line manager is pursuing the relevant procedures. Objectivity is required to resolve the complaint and to bring the matter to a satisfactory conclusion.

Managing managers

It is a commonly-held misconception that managerial performance is more complex and difficult to appraise than teaching. Managers have targets and their performance can be measured. It is often the case that teaching staff have relevant professional teaching qualifications, whereas managers have no formal qualification for their current position. Managers are accountable; they also need training and continual professional development and they need to be managed in the same way as other employees.

Example

'Tom took over as course manager but he never took responsibility for anything. Despite serious warnings the first time round, for example, he failed to register his students with BTEC for the second year running. There was no reason – he just didn't "get round to it". We had to pay a late entry fee for each student out of our section budget. We tried training him, setting him targets and appointing a mentor but he could not – or would not – cope with the demands of course management. We relieved him of this duty. The senior lecturer who took over now manages two courses. She and others in the section feel annoyed that, as a result of Tom's incompetence, they have been rewarded with more work to do.' *Head of Section*

Reflection

As a manager, it was important to take a departmental view. It was clearly beneficial to remove Tom from this role as a damage limitation exercise and to attempt to find him something else. Managers need to recognise, though, that people have strong feelings about justice being seen to be done and work being fairly apportioned. This type of situation provides little incentive for others in the section to be effective course managers.

Issues relating to disagreements or complaints need to be addressed at the time. For the other issues discussed above, such as general performance or attitude, it may be appropriate to address them in a staff development, job review or appraisal meeting.

Appraisal

The typical appraisal system is not about identifying weaknesses. FE managers recognise the need for appraisal to be a positive measure. Interviews are usually undertaken as a vehicle to motivate people and to improve performance, through objective setting. Not all lecturers see appraisal in this light, although the climate is changing. Some remain hostile to any form of judgement on their professional performance.

The main advantage of any system of performance review is that it compels managers to sit down with staff on a one-to-one basis and discuss work-related and staff development issues. Many staff welcome this opportunity to discuss their own needs and how their contribution fits into organisational requirements. If co-ordinated effectively, such interviews can provide invaluable information to contribute to a coherent staff development plan and to the objectives of the college. A skills audit, undertaken by appraisals, may unearth unknown talents and competencies, thereby facilitating redeployment if necessary, rather than redundancy.

Performance appraisal operates in colleges alongside quality systems. However, appraisal is not recognised as contributing to a quality culture. In fact, the management thinkers largely responsible for the quality movement, such as Deming[7] and Crosby[8], whose contributions are discussed in the next chapter, vehemently oppose appraisals. They argue that quality is improved through prevention and not cure. Prevention is brought about through expertise, motivation and commitment and not by appraisal or inspection. Deming identifies the evaluation of an individual's performance through review or merit rating as one of his 'seven deadly diseases' in organisations. Appraisal is inevitably based on measurable outcomes and, as such, it cannot provide a realistic view of an employee's contribution. Rather than improve performance, Deming argues that it focuses attention on the performance rating itself and on short-term solutions, instead of developing pride in one's work. It can also put people in competition with one another, at the expense of encouraging teamwork.

With changes in organisational structures, there is also the question of *who* carries out appraisal. With fewer management layers, more cross-college initiatives and more part-time staff, the principle of the immediate line manager taking responsibility for appraisal becomes unworkable. In many cases managers have too many people to appraise. They may also see some people too infrequently, such as part-time lecturers, to know enough about them. Increasingly, staff report to different people throughout the year, depending on the projects, programmes or course teams they are involved in.

In this type of environment, some, like Fletcher[9] argue that appraisal has outlived its usefulness. He suggests that 'Doubtless the idea of a universally applied, personnel-driven, standard procedure that stays rigidly in place (perhaps kept there by the weight of its own paperwork) for years on end will lumber on in some quarters for a while yet, but its days are certainly numbered.'

Many colleges are only just beginning to link their appraisal systems with strategic objectives and human resource planning. While they are not in a position to abandon appraisal systems, they can take heed of the views expressed above to ensure that appraisal remains a positive and developmental process.

TEAMS

Team roles and team development are discussed in this section.

Work in FE has become much more team focused. It is increasingly unlikely that even lecturers who spend significant amounts of time in the classroom would spend a day without contact with other colleagues, formally or informally. Almost everyone is a member of at least one team, working party or committee.

It is very rare for managers to have the luxury of selecting a team from scratch. In almost all situations, managers have to work with existing groups of individuals. It can be useful, though, to encourage team role awareness and to analyse the composition of a team. There is a considerable amount of material available to help individuals or organisations identify team roles. The most well-known and widely used method is discussed below.

Team roles

Over seven years, Meredith Belbin[10] and his colleagues amassed large amounts of data on team composition and performance. Following their research they were able to predict team performance with a high degree of accuracy. They identified individuals who could make a crucial difference to team performance and named eight types. The Belbin questionnaire is frequently used to help people identify which type most closely approximates to their own personality. The types are described in Figure 4.

How can the Belbin indicator be of value to managers? Ideally, teams should be composed of all these types. Belbin recognised that managers prefer to pick a team composed of the most talented or creative people they know. Often, as he discovered in his research, this does not work. Teams need a finisher, for example, to chase up other members and to keep the team on track in terms of timing. If no-one is clearly identified as a finisher, the situation can be remedied by appointing someone within the team to take on this role.

Balance is the key issue. What is needed in teams is not necessarily well balanced individuals but individuals who balance well with one another. Clearly, having all eight types in a team does not guarantee success, although Belbin argued that *not* having them all and not taking remedial action does increase the likelihood of failure.

It should be noted, however, that a major drawback to any system which relies on questionnaires is that they are based on self-perception. There is also a danger of labelling and stereotyping people once they have completed the questionnaire.

	Description	Positive qualities	Allowable weaknesses
Co-ordinator/ Chairperson	calm; self-controlled confident;	aware of importance of objectives; welcomes contributions on their merit	unlikely to be the most creative team member
Shaper	seeks to impose a shape or pattern on debates and outcomes	energetic and creative; challenges complacency and ineffectiveness	prone to irritation and impatience; can be temperamental
Plant	individualistic; unorthodox	imaginative and intellectual; knowledgeable	may disregard practical issues or protocol
Resources Investigator	extrovert; communicative; enthusiastic	contacts others; explores new territory; responds to challenge	may lose interest after initial enthusiasm
Monitor/ Evaluator	sober; prudent; unemotional	discreet, sensible; encourages team to make balanced decisions	may be uninspiring and unable to motivate others
Implementer; Company Worker	conservative; dutiful; predictable	good organiser; hard working; turns plans and ideas into practice	can be unresponsive to new ideas; may lack flexibility
Team Worker	socially orientated; mild; sensitive	promotes team cohesion	may be indecisive at critical moments
Completer/ Finisher	painstaking; orderly; conscientious; anxious	perfectionism; eye for detail; able to follow-up	may worry about small issues and be reluctant to let go

Figure 4 Belbin's classifications

Team development

Teams grow and develop. They tend to have a dynamic of their own. As a manager it is useful to recognise the stages of team development. While no model can accurately reflect the complexities of team dynamics, models are useful in providing an opportunity to understand a little more about the team and its progress.

Tuckman's model[11] is particularly helpful. It identifies four stages: forming, storming, norming, performing.

- **Forming** This is the initial adjustment period and it is often one of misunderstanding and mistrust, particularly as the team is likely to be 'thrown' together, rather than deliberately chosen.
- **Storming** At this point in its development, conflicts and tensions come to the fore, as the team tries to cope with the pressure involved.
- **Norming** As working procedures are agreed and ground rules are established, closer working relations develop and people are able to discuss issues in an objective manner.
- **Performing** With a high degree of commitment and flexibility, group synergy is achieved.

Example

'As the four Programme Managers in the Faculty, we met on a weekly basis for over a year with the Dean. It just never worked. We didn't argue but we never seemed to achieve anything. We were all quite similar – all strong characters, hard working and committed. No-one ever admitted, though, that it wasn't working. Recently, Graham left and Liz has moved to another Faculty. Two of the programme areas have merged and so Graham and Liz have been replaced by one new person, Sean. The dynamics are much better now. We're really getting things done.' *Programme Manager*

Reflection

Some groups do not even reach the storming stage. With hindsight, more time should have been spent analysing the composition of this team. The Dean recognised that the team was not functioning but failed to take any action.

Groups do not always work methodically through each stage, as is illustrated by the example above. Some reach but never leave the storming stage. Others move forwards and then backwards. If the stages are recognised, however, it is possible to take certain actions. During the forming stage, it is helpful to encourage the team members to get to know one another and to examine the function and purpose of the team, as well as identify existing skills and knowledge. It is preferable at this stage to avoid jumping to conclusions too quickly or imposing immediate changes. At the storming stage, conflict needs to be handled positively and constructively and openness and feedback should be encouraged. This stage cannot be rushed as it takes time to build trust. Success in both the norming and performing stages can be celebrated, while still maintaining regular progress reviews.

Another description of the way in which teams move towards maturity is provided by W R Bion's model[12]. Bion suggested the following 'as if' behaviour types:

- **Dependency** Members behave 'as if' they cannot make their own decisions but need a strong leader to take the initiative.

- **Fight/flight** 'As if' under threat, members overreact to a perceived threat from another department or section.
- **Pairings** Individuals join forces with others and teams then behave 'as if' the impact of pairs or sub-groups is highly influential.
- **Maturity** The team is fully developed and can work effectively.

As with Belbin's model, these stages can provide a starting point to think about what needs to be done to move a team through its development stages in order to ensure that it reaches the mature, performing stage.

Context, task and outcome

The models discussed above focus on how team members work together and the sequence of developmental stages that a team passes through. Herriot and Pemberton[13] (1996) argue that these two elements, though useful, are insufficient to understand or to manage teams.

Their own model includes elements of context, tasks, processes, roles and outcomes. They argue that to concentrate on team processes in isolation from the task and its context is meaningless. The nature of the task determines the way in which it is tackled and it is the organisational context which sets the task. The organisational context has an impact on the processes used. People take on different roles but a team is judged, ultimately, not by the way in which people work together but by the outcome.

Four processes are identified by Herriot and Pemberton as being necessary for teams to achieve their task:

- achieving motivation and momentum
- defining issues and getting ideas
- managing the boundaries
- evaluating progress and outcomes.

Each of these four team processes is dependent on particular roles being played and four general, broad-ranging roles are identified. They are traditionalists, visionaries, catalysts and loyalists. Each individual prefers one of these roles and an under or over representation of the people willing to play these roles profoundly affects task achievement.

SELF

To improve the way in which they manage others, people need to reflect on how they manage themselves. In this section, time management, diaries, to-do lists and priorities are discussed as well as stress management.

Time management

Almost everything in colleges that can be measured is measured – staff qualifications, room utilisation, retention rates, financial performance, students' examination results and lecturers' teaching hours, to name but a few. What is rarely measured and costed, however, is managers' time.

Many people in FE complain of 'not enough hours in the day', overwork and excessive pressure. In order to improve time management, where possible, a comprehensive audit of where the time actually goes is recommended. This involves keeping a detailed log for a day, a week or ideally longer. Those who are most in need of improved time management skills are likely to argue that they do not have the time to keep a log! On the other hand, they will readily spend time analysing timetables, where they are looking at other people's time, or budgets where they are examining the resource implications of decisions, because they feel that these tasks form part of their job, whereas managing their own time does not.

From the completed log, the main time-wasters and ways of tackling them can be identified. In most cases, the time-wasters fall into a few categories which are usually poor planning, poor organisation, ineffective meetings and interruptions.

- Poor planning is often characterised by not briefing others sufficiently; being insufficiently prepared for meetings; failing to read important documentation or having to concentrate on important tasks when feeling exhausted.
- Poor organisation may be highlighted by an untidy desk; failing to deal with problems before they escalate; no system for incoming paperwork or recognised system for certain procedures.
- Ineffective meetings do not achieve anything; they have an insufficiently clear focus; they are poorly chaired; they often start late and run over time.
- Interruptions result from always responding to colleagues who want a word; students who need to see you; ad hoc meetings with line managers, distraught parents, students or employers or visiting verifiers, inspectors or governors.

Tackling the time-wasters may involve an initial investment of even more time.

Example

'We have lots of visiting lecturers in this section and also student teachers. It takes ages showing people how to get copying done, explaining how they put in a claim, which computers they can use, where the keys are kept etc. What is worse, I know that they do not like asking me or any of the section managers, as they recognise we're all incredibly busy. So I produced a small handbook, listing the question and giving the answers. It was worth the effort. It hasn't taken away the 'human' element. I still welcome people but I no longer have to go through all the nitty gritty.' *Head of School*

Reflection

This Head of School recognised that she was spending significant amounts of time providing the same information over and over again to different people. The handbook took up a considerable amount of her valuable time but she recognised it was a worthwhile investment. It saved her time and resulted in a more professional and systematic approach. Other managers in the college are currently adapting the handbook for use in their schools.

Responsibility

Taking responsibility for, and controlling, work helps to prevent the feeling of overload. There is a temptation in FE – given the variety of activities and the demands – to simply react and to take on everything that is thrown your way. Being busy, though, is not necessarily the same as being effective. This approach can prevent managers from setting realistic goals and being proactive. While it may not be appropriate to reject work requested of you by your own line manager, it is important to fit such tasks into your own framework and to prioritise them according to the extent to which they meet your work-related goals.

Example

'When I was a Head of Department I more or less knew what I had to do. When I took on this new cross-college role, I felt totally swamped for the first year. I just reacted to whatever came my way. The Principal used to send me stuff with my name on the top right hand corner. Other people did the same. I felt like a dumping ground. I worked incredibly hard. When it came to my appraisal, though, I couldn't clearly identify what I had actually achieved. In the appraisal, we set specific targets and I have since learnt (the hard way) about the importance of relating jobs to achieving my targets. This helps me to prioritise, delegate or simply not do certain jobs. It also makes me think about action *I* should be initiating.' *Learning Support Manager*

Reflection

In this case the manager could not manage his time effectively until he clarified where he was going and how he was going to get there.

In setting goals, it is important to remember that they need to be specific, attainable and realistic but – at the same time – sufficiently challenging to maximise the feeling of satisfaction when realised. A useful acronym is
> SMART
>> Specific
>> Measurable
>> Attainable
>> Realistic
>> Timed

Diaries

Entries in diaries are often reactions to other people's demands. Managers are most likely to use diaries to remind themselves of meetings, teaching times and visits. They are less likely to use diaries as a time management tool. This strategy involves allocating time in the diary for specific, self imposed tasks as shown in Figure 5.

0900	*deal with mail*
1000	*timetabling*
1100	
1200	
1300	*lunch*
1400	*write staff dev't plan*
1500	
1600	
1700	
1800	
1900	
2000	
2100	

Figure 5 Using a diary as a time management tool

Entering a finish time as well as start time for each activity, even if it is externally imposed, and allocating specific times in the diary for work that you initiate, are useful techniques for developing and improving time management skills.

Prioritising

There is usually a temptation to tackle the enjoyable jobs first. Delaying the least enjoyable tasks (for example, dealing with complaints or poor performance as discussed earlier) can result in the development of more serious problems.

Similarly, urgent tasks take priority but this may be at the expense of important work. Being able to distinguish between important and urgent is a key requirement of successful time management. Urgent tasks have clear deadlines, often imposed by others. If there is an accident, fight or break in, it has to be dealt with immediately. If someone is leaving at the end of this week, a farewell has to be arranged before that person goes. Deadlines for bids must be met or there is a possibility of losing money.

Important tasks may have long term deadlines or possibly none at all. Examples may include: planning for next year, evaluating the feedback of a course or project just undertaken, re-writing a course handbook, re-organising a filing system, tackling problems such as students' lateness or organising staff development sessions on classroom management. It is up to the manager concerned to set deadlines and prioritise according to specified aims. If not, the tasks do not get done, the problems may deteriorate or they eventually fall into the urgent stage, by which time they have to be undertaken in a hurry and, as a consequence, may not be completed to a satisfactory standard.

To-do lists

Making a to-do list is common practice for many people. The effectiveness of such lists varies. One method is to divide your paper or computer screen into a grid as shown in Figure 6.

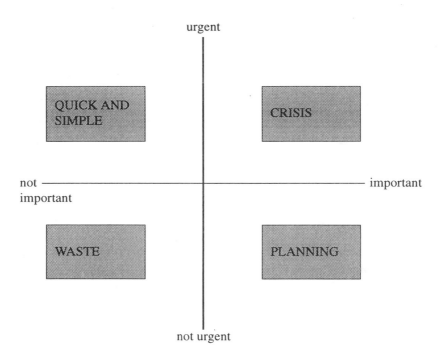

Figure 6 The time grid

As a job is entered on to the list, the user must think about which of the categories it belongs to. This step alone can be helpful. There are four options. Jobs can be:

important and urgent	–	CRISIS
important and not urgent	–	PLANNING
urgent and not important	–	QUICK AND SIMPLE
not urgent and not important	–	WASTE

Those in *quick and simple* can be done quickly, without too much effort or time. If jobs are put into *waste*, you need to ask whether they should be done at all. Those jobs in *crisis* need to be attended to first because of tight deadlines. Those in *planning* must be tackled regularly. The temptation is to leave the planning tasks because they do not have immediate deadline dates. If left, though, they start to move into *crisis* and there is then a danger of entering into a cycle whereby all activities are urgent, leaving no time to address the planning ones, which in turn become urgent. This state is commonly referred to as 'crisis management'. An example list is shown in Figure 7.

QUICK AND SIMPLE	CRISIS
tell reception about tonight	*arrange cover for this afternoon's lesson (JB rang in ill)*

WASTE	PLANNING
	quality review documents – read, make notes, action, reports
	prepare appraisal material
	job description for new post
	check capital bid with JK
	organise catering for advisory board
	send out advisory board invitations
	arrange staff don't session on key skills

Figure 7 An example of using the time grid

Stress

Most people recognise when they are stressed. Stress is not, in itself, destructive. Pressure, in itself, does not constitute stress. Stress is generated by an individual's response to an 'unacceptable' level of pressure. The key is to acquire the right balance. Too little pressure can be a source of stress, leading to apathy and boredom. Some pressure is beneficial and, in an ideal situation, people enjoy responding to pressure in a stimulated way and tend to perform extremely well. Once the balance begins to tip, though, people experience the unpleasant feeling of stress – the tension between the pressure placed upon them and their ability to cope with it.

As well as managing their own stress levels, managers in FE, as elsewhere, need to recognise the symptoms in others and to provide appropriate support. Typical symptoms include loss of concentration, indecision, snapping at students and colleagues, losing work, going to classes and meetings unprepared, making mistakes and poor judgements.

It is recognised that effective time management can help reduce stress. Planning the workload to include regular lunch breaks and to avoid the need to take work home on a regular basis will help, as will exercise, relaxation and care over diet.

CONCLUSION

Although it sounds like a truism, it is worth repeating that people are a college's most important resource. The staff represent a significant investment in the future performance of the college. In FE, too frequently, staff are seen as a major expense rather than as a valuable resource. In most cases, multi-skilling has involved an increase in workload for a core of staff and for others, on the periphery, it has meant greater job insecurity with short-term contracts or part-time and fractional work. The management of people in this context provides a real challenge to those in FE. As a manager, learning to empower and motivate others, as well as oneself, not only makes individuals work more effectively; it also helps to unblock the whole organisation, removing the restrictions standing between a college and its goals. To harness the full potential of everyone in a college may require a major cultural upheaval. The inter-related issues of culture and change are explored in the next chapter. Quality programmes, also discussed in the next chapter, cannot be implemented unless organisations gain commitment and liberate people's abilities rather than restrict their autonomy.

REFERENCES AND NOTES

[1] Mintzberg, H (1996) 'Ten ideas to rile everyone who cares about management' *Harvard Business Review* July–August.

[2] Maslow, A (1943) 'A Theory of Human Motivation' *Psychological Review* Vol 50 no 4.

[3] McGregor, D (1966) *Leadership and Motivation* MIT Press.

[4] Kindler, H S (1988) *Managing Disagreement Constructively* Kogan Page.

[5] Arvey and Jones (1985) 'The use of discipline in organisational settings: a framework for future research' in Cummins and Straw (ed) *Research in organisational behaviour* Vol 7, JAI Press.

[6] Nicholls, A (1995) 'Legal action looms for one in six colleges' *Furthering Education* 9 Winter 95:96.

[7] Deming, W E (1986) *Out of the Crisis* Cambridge University Press.

[8] Crosby, P (1995) *Reflections on Quality* McGraw Hill.

[9] Fletcher, C (1996) 'Appraisal: an idea whose time has gone?' in Billsberry, J (ed) *The Effective Manager: Perspectives and Illustrations* Sage Publications.

[10] Belbin, M (1993) *Team Roles at Work* Butterworth Heinemann.

[11] Tuckman, B W (1963) 'Development sequence in small groups' *Psychological Bulletin* 384–399.

[12] Bion, W R (1994) in Fraser, A and Neville, S *Team Building* The Industrial Society.

[13] Herriot, P and Pemberton, C (1996) 'Teams: old myths and a new model' in Billsberry, J (ed) *The Effective Manager: Perspectives and Illustrations* Sage Publications.

CHAPTER 2

Managing Operations

INTRODUCTION

The key themes of change, culture and quality central to this chapter all affect the management of operations, as well as one another. Each theme is discussed in turn, with examples from colleges.

CHANGE

Coping with change and working in seemingly chaotic conditions has become a way of life in FE. As discussed in the Introductory Chapter, much of the emphasis on organisation and management literature of the late eighties was on change, responsiveness and flexibility. The management of change is now recognised as an important management competence.

Even before the eighties, however, Alvin Toffler[1] argued that the rate of change is now out of control and that modern society is potentially 'doomed to a massive adaptational breakdown'. He believed that there is a limit to the amount of change humans can handle and he talks about 'future shock' in describing the stress and disorientation experienced during times of change.

Organisational structure

FE colleges are in a constant state of change and, to a large extent, survival depends on their ability to adjust to these changes. The challenge is to ensure that colleges are stable enough to maintain organisational effectiveness but, at the same time, are sufficiently flexible to adapt to the pressures for change.

Many leading management theorists over the last forty years have written about the limitations of 'traditional' organisational structures and styles to deal with turbulence and uncertainty. It has been recognised that bureaucracies may be suitable as a form of organisation to cope with stability and routine, simple structures and standardised jobs and skills. They are less able to adapt, however, to rapid and unpredictable change, to the diversity of skills required and to more participative management styles.

In describing different organisational structures and styles, Burns and Stalker[2] differentiated between *mechanistic* and *organic* management systems. Toffler[3] names the new, flexible organisations *adhocracies*, while Kanter[4] distinguishes between conventional *segmentalist* structures and the new change-oriented *integrative* structures.

Example

'Our marketing research highlighted that there was a need for a short, intensive course in electronics. We spent a lot of time discussing it with the department who could deliver it, only to find out that there was not enough time left in the year to organise an internal validation, let alone get the course externally validated. There are loads of forms to fill in and a course proposal has to go before the department's Board of Studies, which doesn't meet again until next year. We have to leave it now until the following year but I'm sure we've missed the boat.' *Marketing Manager*

Reflection

The requirement for flexibility and responsiveness has to be balanced against the need for planning and quality assurance. In this case, the structure of the organisation and the rigidity of the procedures involved did not allow for the development of this new course at relatively short notice.

Aspects of the organisational structure in a college can hinder – if not prevent – the implementation of key objectives. Often, new functions emerge and they are not allocated to a specific post. The work of GNVQ coordinators, for example, cuts across traditional subject boundaries. Some GNVQ coordinators feel frustrated that, because of the organisational structure and associated lines of communication, they cannot implement any changes on a college-wide basis, particularly in colleges which have strong, semi-autonomous departments. If they cannot 'overrule' departmental practice, they are unable to do their job effectively.

In many colleges there is resistance to the establishment of central or common systems and this is discussed more fully in Chapter 3, in relation to bidding for funds. As colleges move towards central services – such as admissions, marketing and learning resource centres – the organisational structure changes, as does the balance between 'academic' and 'support' staff. The demarcation of roles between lecturers, instructors, technicians and counsellors, for example, is beginning to break down. This multi-skilling of the workforce, discussed in Chapter 1, may be positive if it is geared towards the customers' needs and if it provides people with new skills and more varied employment. However, it can cause considerable tension in relation to workload, salaries and status.

Middle managers

As commercial and industrial organisations became more flexible and adaptive it was the middle manager who suffered, as a result of 'delayering'. Middle managers have been portrayed in recent literature as frustrated, disillusioned and stuck in the middle of a hierarchy in dreary jobs[5] with little hope of career advancement[6]. The very term 'middle manager' has become associated with outmoded organisations. James Quinn sees them as an obstacle to change: 'Just as Gorbachev could change the top level of the USSR and establish grassroots support for change quickly – but could not move the middle layers of his bureaucracy – Western middle managers resist radical changes endlessly'[7].

Not all researchers or writers agree with the view that middle managers are about to become extinct. Nonaka and Takeuchi espouse a 'middle-up-down' management structure[8], with middle managers playing the key role, working as a bridge between the visionary ideals of the top and the frequently chaotic realities confronted by those at the front line. Mintzberg agrees with this view but argues that tops and bottoms are inappropriate metaphors for organisations[9]. He presents the metaphor of a circle, with what he calls *central* management in the middle and others around the outer edges, developing producing and delivering products and services. While they can see their own small segment clearly, managers at the centre can see all around the circle but not particularly clearly because they are distant from the operations. There is, therefore, still a need for middle managers who can see the outer edge and then swing around and talk about it to those at the centre.

Colleges frequently undergo re-structuring, often to coincide with the arrival of a new principal or as a result of redundancies. At the time of incorporation, rather than following the trend to delayer, in many cases, colleges moved in the opposite direction. Specialists were employed at management level to deal with aspects of the college's work previously undertaken by the LEA – for example, personnel, estates and finance. More recently, however, re-structuring has tended to move colleges away from a strictly departmental structure to facilitate cross-college fertilisation and activity.

Vision and mission

Creating a vision owned and shared by the people within an organisation is often cited as a route to effective management and success. Senge writes: 'Without a pull towards some goal which people truly want to achieve, the forces in support of the status quo can be overwhelming. Vision establishes an overarching goal'[10].

Many people in colleges remain cynical on this issue. The notion of giving one's allegiance to institutional core purposes or values rather than to one's profession is seen to be more appropriate for a large multinational.

The vision is usually expressed in the college's mission statement and in the strategic plan. This, however, can be the 'theoretical' vision. Often the mission statement is simply bolted on to the college and ignored when it comes to action. It is seen as something required by the FEFC, the TECs and governors and of no real interest to staff or students. To be of value, it has to be truly owned and shared and managers need to consider every action they take in the light of the college's mission.

One college principal[11] explains 'What we are trying to do . . . is to turn (the college) into a learning organisation. We were doing so long before the term became fashionable, coming to it from the drive to be student-centred, learner-focused, corporate in the sense of shared mission. The British are not very easy with some of this "vision" stuff, but we need to get over our collective discomfort. Genuinely shared vision can transform organisations.'

Leadership and management

An organisation's vision usually emanates from the top or, to use Mintzberg's metaphor, from centre management. The term 'leader' is rarely used in FE as it has connotations of military dictators or of an elite group from privileged backgrounds. Leading, however, is one aspect of managing and there is an expectation by those being managed that leadership should be exercised.

Many people in FE perceive leaders or managers as foes rather than friends. They perceive them as 'collaborators' with the new forces of managerialism invading the autonomy traditionally enjoyed in FE. They may even be seen as failed academics, using their managerial role to undermine professional values.

Leadership style is often described on a continuum from autocratic at one end to democratic at the other end. Contemporary theories on leadership fall into the contingency or 'best fit' approach. They argue that no particular style is more successful than any other. Leadership styles need to differ according to the context. They have to take into account other variables such as the task and the group.

Most writers on management theory argue that a participative and supportive style is generally more effective. Such a style draws on the ideas of others, involves them in the decision-making process and thereby has a greater likelihood of commitment. Autocratic management, on the other hand, can stifle creativity, fail to use valuable expertise and may de-motivate people. It can be highly effective, though, when decisions are required urgently, when the leader is the most knowledgeable and experienced person and when others fail to reach an agreement.

Four leadership dimensions are identified by Marsh (1992)[12] and ideally leaders bring each of these four aspects together. They are:

- **Symbolic** The leader embodies symbolically the whole college and represents the institution by presenting its corporate image and by obtaining resources.
- **Political** The leader handles effectively the demands of all relevant constituencies.
- **Managerial** The leader, as chief executive, performs the standard tasks of management as identified by Drucker[13]: setting objectives, organising, motivating and communicating, measuring and developing people.
- **Academic** The leader is the 'professional', deciding when, where and how to intervene to strengthen academic structures.

The extent to which these four dimensions are visible in different educational leaders varies considerably. 'The real test of leadership,' writes Bass[14], 'lies not in the personality or behaviour of the leaders, but in the performance of the groups they lead.'

Change agents

As a manager, you may be caught in the middle. You may have had no involvement in a specific change and yet you are responsible for implementing it in your college, department or section. The change is likely to have been presented as a *fait accompli*. It may relate to any aspect of work: the curriculum (for example, the move to competence based programmes); new employment conditions (for example, working to new contracts) or finance (for example, changing from the familiar concept of 'full time equivalent' student numbers to the calculation of target units).

Principals and senior management teams may spend considerable amounts of time discussing strategic issues but place less emphasis on how to handle the transition from the old to the new. The college strategic plan, for example, is likely to include a number of new goals, targets and outcomes without sufficient reference to the implementation period. As a result, middle managers, in particular, may feel 'squeezed'. Often there is pressure from above to implement changes without the necessary information or guidance and, on the other hand, resistance from below by an angry, frustrated and confused team.

Example

'I was being pushed to cut student contact hours even more. I knew why and I knew all about the financial problems. Senior management were talking about providing more in the way of learning support for students but there was nothing concrete and no chance of anything being in place by September. What would happen in the intervening period? The staff were, quite rightly, furious when I told them about it.' *Head of Section*

Reflection

This is an example which is likely to be familiar to people in many colleges. In this case, the manager recognised the need for the change and did, in fact, have some involvement in the decision, through his participation on various committees. As a manager, he needed to take responsibility to implement the necessary changes but gaining the support of his section was extremely difficult.

The changes experienced by managers in FE are often not initiated by them, although they can usually anticipate them. A typical initial reaction is one of helplessness and blame, with a longing to return to the security of the past. It is not uncommon to hear comments like: 'It's government policy.' 'Nothing I can do.' 'No one asked us.' 'All colleges are the same.'

The role of the manager becomes one of change agent. The change agent needs to direct energy away from anger, frustration and feelings of powerlessness towards identifying new opportunities. At the time, this may seem difficult, if not impossible. Taking control and thinking creatively are critical aspects of effective change management.

Example

'There was a break-in in the college and all the computers in our section were stolen. It was heartbreaking. It seemed like the last straw, near the end of a very stressful year. It meant all change – we had to re-do the timetables, cancel time-constrained assignments, and get lecturers preparing theory sessions. The students were really fed up. Instead of despairing, though, we took the opportunity to get together as a department and re-assess our needs. We planned what we would buy with the insurance money. Some of the computers were quite old and, with the cost of computers going down, in real terms, we ended up with much better hardware and software.' *Head of Department of Computing*

Reflection

At this time of the externally imposed, sudden change, the Head of Department focused on the opportunities the break-in presented, rather than the negative aspects. The chance to participate in the decision-making process brought people closer together.

Communicating change

At a time of change, open communication is vital. Delivering unsettling news to people is an unpleasant aspect of a manager's job and often managers will avoid doing so for as long as possible. As a result, people rely on rumours and informal networks which, in turn, serve to increase anxieties.

The most effective form of communicating change involves talking to people formally and informally, encouraging questions, telling the truth and allowing people to express their feelings. Memos and newsletters are useful as follow-ups but not as substitutes for face-to-face contact. (Communication is discussed more fully in Chapter 4.)

Example

'The college had serious financial problems. We were given a budget for our Faculty and I could see immediately that it would cover staff salaries but not a lot else. Rumours were rife about redundancies and so I decided to hold a staff meeting as soon as possible. I simply presented the figures I had, admitted that I did not have any magic answers and responded to questions as honestly as I could.' *Director of Media and Design*

Reflection

Staff took considerable comfort in knowing the facts and being able to differentiate fact from fiction. The Director was not afraid to admit that he did not have all the answers. He encouraged suggestions from his team as to how they might manage in the coming year.

While communicating the information is important, it is not enough, of course, simply to tell people about change and to assume that they will therefore take it on board. Working in a learning environment, people in colleges are only too familiar with the idea that students do not learn simply by being given information. They need guidance, support and encouragement. In the same way, staff need help if they are to change their behaviour.

Responses to change

Most people, including those implementing the change, have strong responses to moving from the familiar to the unknown. It is not just a question of resistance, but also one of loss. Even adjusting to a positive change such as a promotion, can involve the loss of a familiar work pattern.

Example

'In the re-organisation, Sheena had to move site and work with a new team. I didn't understand why she got so stressed. We had discussed it and she was willing to do it. In fact, she saw working with the level three team, as opposed to the level two team, as a sort of promotion.' *Programme Leader*

Reflection

There were several types of loss involved in this change. Sheena may have been concerned about competence – could she manage this new team and new course? She 'lost' her old relationships and contacts and, most notably, there was a loss of territory. In giving up her old course, she relinquished an area that 'belonged' to her. As well as this psychological territory, she also gave up her familiar physical space.

While reactions vary, there are recognisable stages which people go through when confronted with change, as illustrated in Figure 8.

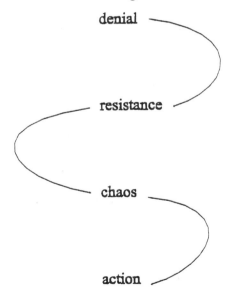

Figure 8 Stages when confronting change

The first is denial. At this point, information is ignored and people carry on as normal. In the second stage – resistance – people begin to express anger and anxiety and to think about their own position. During this stage, people feel the need to discuss the 'crisis' with colleagues and to share views and concerns. The third stage is chaos. This stage is characterised by frenetic activity and outbursts of energy but also a lack of coherence. New ideas are tossed around, new ways of working and adapting are hastily discussed and responsibilities are questioned and reviewed. In the final stage, people demonstrate that they are ready to commit themselves to an agreed way forward.

Example

'When we first presented the student retention figures, broken down by course, they were simply ignored by the programme managers. When pushed for comments, however, they got angry, asking questions like "who needs to know?" Then they insisted that the figures were all wrong. Even if they *were* right, there was nothing we could do about it. Weren't *all* colleges having the same problem? Weren't some colleges even worse? Finally, people began to accept the fact that our retention figures were poor and that we had to do something about it. There was an amazing flurry of activity. People came up with all sorts of new programme ideas, particularly in relation to short, incoming generating courses. Most didn't come to anything. We are now just about settling down to tackling the problem in a co-ordinated and systematic way.' *Principal*

Reflection

In this example, it is possible to clearly identify the various stages of denial, resistance, chaos and action.

Resistance to change

As a manager, it is helpful to recognise these stages. To confront denial, it is important to emphasise that the changes *will* take place and to encourage discussion about possible actions to be taken. During the resistance stage, managers need to listen and acknowledge the concerns and anxieties of their team. During the chaos stage, it may be necessary to respond to all ideas and suggestions but also to identify priorities and short-term goals. In the final stage, it is possible to start recognising people's commitment and contribution and to concentrate on more long-term plans.

Most advice on the implementation and management of change revolves around variations on the themes of participation, consultation and involvement. These were discussed in Chapter 1 in relation to motivation and empowerment. There are, however, more manipulative approaches.

Kanter[15] for example, talks about 'power skills' to help managers overcome resistance and apathy to new ideas. She suggests the following techniques:

- wait them out (they may go away)
- wear them out (keep arguing and pushing)
- appeal to a higher authority (you had better agree because he/she does)
- invite them in (let them join the party)
- send emissaries (get friends in to talk to them)
- display support (have 'your' people present and active at meetings)
- reduce the stakes (alter parts of the proposals which are particularly damaging)

- warn them off (let them know senior management are on your side)
- remember (only afterwards does an innovation look like the right thing to have done).

Manipulative techniques may work well in certain circumstances but they run the risk of being successful in the short term only. They may also be resented by those who are subjected to them.

A useful technique to identify and reduce resistance is force field analysis, as illustrated in Figure 9.

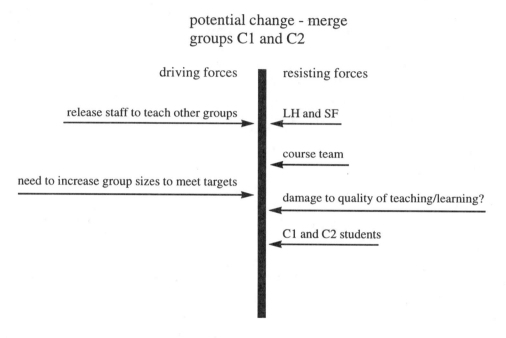

Figure 9 An example of force field analysis

The steps involved in this process are:

- on one side of a line, list the forces which are driving the change and on the other side, list those forces which are resisting change
- represent each force with an arrow indicating its influence by the length of the line (for example, the longer the line, the greater the resistance or the driving force)
- identify ways to tackle the resisting forces, dealing first with the longest lines.

A well known and frequently used technique is the SWOT analysis. SWOT is an acronym for Strengths, Weaknesses, Opportunities and Threats. It has become a commonplace tool of strategic planning in FE and it can also be used effectively to analyse a potential next step in a change process. The idea is to list all strengths, weaknesses, opportunities and threats under the appropriate headings. The strengths and weaknesses reflect an internal audit, while the threats and opportunities concentrate on the external environmental context. The aim of the exercise is to maximise strengths, minimise weaknesses, reduce threats and build on opportunities.

Change rarely takes place in an orderly, structured fashion. Whatever the trigger for the change, the easiest option is usually to modify or tinker with existing systems, structures and processes. Another option, though, is to start afresh, using the 'technique' called business process re-engineering (BPR), as discussed in the Introductory Chapter. This option, with a case study from FE, is explored more fully in Chapter 4, in relation to management information systems.

A further option is to procure the services of external consultants. It is often suggested that colleges fail to draw on the wide range of expertise which exists within institutions. Those teaching systems analysis or computing, for example, rarely get consulted about their own college's management information systems and management lecturers teaching quality may not be involved in their college's own quality system. More credibility is given to the view of external consultants. The main advantage of looking outside of the college is that external consultants can comment freely without having to be concerned about internal politics and they can view problems afresh without the 'baggage' of the past.

The ways in which the management of change is undertaken depend, to a large extent, on the culture of the college.

CULTURE

It is not uncommon to hear discussions about 'culture changes' in colleges, particularly since incorporation. In some cases, Principals and senior managers make explicit their aim to change the normally accepted values shared by employees of the college. Culture is an abstract concept; it is about the way things are done and the way in which people behave. It is a unique combination of values, beliefs and behavioural patterns which characterise the way in which groups and individuals within a college work together.

One Principal[16] is attempting to shift the culture of his college from political to rational, from 'differentiation, dissonance, competition, bidding, blaming . . . to interpretation, cohesion, analysis, planning, negotiation.'

While a 'corporate' college culture may be actively promoted, the underpinning culture is often less tangible. Individuals may resist 'buying into' these corporate values and systems.

It is frequently the case that different cultures within a college exist side by side – in different sections, departments or sites. Frequently, departments or sections actively strive for their own way of operating.

Example

'I did my teaching practice in two different departments and they were on different sites. It was as if they were totally separate organisations. One was really efficient and business-like and the other was very laid back and disorganised. The systems for everything – registers, keys, photocopiers etc – were completely different.' *Trainee FE Teacher*

Reflection

The cultures on these two sites were quite different. This was due largely to the fact that, until a merger a few years earlier, they had, in fact, been different colleges. Other factors, though, were of importance, for example, the management styles of the two Heads of Department.

Four types of organisational culture have been identified by Handy[17]: power culture; role culture; person culture; and task culture. Each type is discussed in turn.

Power culture

In this culture, power rests with a central figure of authority or group of key individuals. In the case of colleges, this is usually the Principal and members of the senior management team. Decisions are taken somewhat arbitrarily, rather than in accordance with logic or procedure. The main strength of organisations with power cultures is that they can react quickly but the direction they take depends on the person – or people – in control.

Example

'The Principal, a classicist, stepped in personally to stop us withdrawing the Latin A Level. Even though it only ever recruits a few people and she herself issued a memo to all HODs saying we can't run classes of under fourteen!' *Head of General Studies*

Reflection

This is a clear example of power culture. Selecting a subject of personal interest, the Principal chose to overrule the decision of the Head of Department, despite known organisational rules and procedures.

Role culture

This type of culture is better known as a bureaucracy. The organisation is structured according to functions or expertise, for example departments relating to academic or vocational disciplines. Each department may be strong in its own right but is co-ordinated by a group of senior managers by means of written rules and procedures. In this culture, roles and job descriptions, as opposed to people, are important. The organisation's efficiency therefore depends less on the quality of individuals and more on the rationality of the allocation of work and responsibility.

As discussed earlier in this chapter, the success of a role culture, or bureaucracy, depends upon a stable environment. It tends to be slow to perceive the need for change and slow to change even if the need is acknowledged.

Person culture

In the person culture the purpose of the organisation is to serve the individual.

Such organisations are rare although in colleges it is possible to identify people – less frequently now – whose behaviour and attitudes reveal a preference for this type of culture. Identifying factors are considerable personal freedom and autonomy and a high degree of flexibility. In some cases, lecturers in FE exercise this freedom by working outside of their teaching. They may, for example, run a business or undertake private consultancy. Although these activities may add interest or value to the college, that is not the motive for pursuing them.

Example

'Anthony was working as a technician but in fact he was using the college as an office to run his own business. He was always using the phone and the fax. As well as buying and selling computers, he was also running a travel business, selling cheap flights. Not only did people turn a blind eye to this but they actually bought tickets from him!' *Dean of Faculty*

Reflection

In this extreme case, the behaviour was frowned upon but accepted for many years. Nevertheless, Anthony was subsequently dismissed.

Task culture

The task culture emphasises the accomplishment of a task or project. To do this, the organisation brings together appropriately qualified people in a team and allocates resources to them. Team members enjoy mutual respect within the team, based on their skills, knowledge and experience rather than seniority. The task culture can be highly adaptable. Groups are formed for a specific purpose and can be reformed, abandoned or continued.

Example

'To develop the multimedia course we got together a team from across the college – from performing arts, media, photography, technology and computing. Although it was difficult to arrange times for us all to meet, everyone was really keen and we worked well together.' *Lecturer in Technology*

Reflection

Many curriculum developments do not fit neatly into the departmental structures in colleges. Cross college initiatives, drawing on the expertise of a range of lecturers, like the one described above, are examples of task culture.

The limiting factors of the task culture are, firstly, that the common vision of the organisation may be overlooked and, secondly, it becomes difficult to ensure availability of individuals within traditional hierarchical and departmental organisational structures.

Culture changes have come about in FE, in many cases as a result of the implementation of quality programmes. The concept of quality is discussed below.

QUALITY

Almost all college strategic plans make reference to 'quality provision' but few attempt to define it. In the commercial and industrial world, quality is usually taken to mean that which best satisfies and exceeds the wants and needs of the customer. In FE, it is more difficult to use this type of definition as it is not necessarily clear who the 'customer' is. Customers may be students, parents, employers, government, the community, higher education establishments or indeed all tax payers. In his report 'Quality and Standards in Further Education in England 94/5'[18] the Chief Inspector of the FEFC, describes quality in the following way:

Quality is interpreted primarily in terms of the student experience and can be judged in terms of:
- the skill with which the educational and training processes are managed
- the extent to which the experience meets students' needs
- the care with which students are placed on appropriate courses on which they are likely to succeed
- the academic and pastoral support and guidance provided for students
- the specialist knowledge and pedagogic skills displayed by teachers
- the fitness for purpose of the learning environment
- the range and appropriateness of the physical resources used to support teaching and learning.

The report goes on to state that 'high quality is an aspiration; quality, although not measurable, is amenable to professional judgement; and comparisons of quality between institutions must take account of the differences in mission and values'.

Taking what might appear to be a more commercially orientated view of quality, one college principal[19] describes quality as 'customer delight rather than customer satisfaction. It is about total staff involvement rather than hierarchical, top-down system imposition'.

Recognising that most theory about quality originates from manufacturing, many people in colleges dislike the idea of comparing educational processes to the manufacture of goods. There are clearly major differences. In colleges, unlike manufacturing, the 'producer' and 'consumer' meet face-to-face. FE colleges are not even like other service organisations such as banks, restaurants or solicitors. In a college, the service intensity is very high. Customers do not just drop in for a meal or to withdraw money. A great deal more time in colleges is spent at the 'delivery interface'. Students may spend two years, or longer, attending courses.

Example

'The Patel twins were renowned. We'd all taught them. They both did the Intermediate and then went on to the Advanced and then the HND. One had to re-take a year on the National and the other re-took a year on the HND so they ended up finishing at the same time. They were at college for six years and we all got to know them quite well.'
Head of Construction Studies

Reflection

These 'customers', although not typical, reflect the degree of service intensity in colleges.

FE is different in other ways, too. Unlike a conventional product, a poor lesson cannot be sent back or repaired. Indeed, a student may not recognise it as a poor lesson until the end of the course, when he or she is unable to achieve the intended outcome. Similarly, a traditional lesson cannot be stored for future use. If the student fails to turn up, that particular lesson is gone for good.

Of significance in FE colleges is the fact that senior – and often middle – managers do not usually deliver the service. Those most experienced and those likely to be most concerned about quality are generally remote from the customer. It is critical, therefore, for managers to ensure that all staff are fully aware of the level of service which is expected of them.

Example

'If we appoint someone for any post nowadays we have to go through the whole advertising, interview and selection procedures, which takes months. We're really fussy – quite rightly – about all the usual things: qualifications, experience, equal opportunities etc. However, if I need someone to teach the AAT evening class students next week, I can employ any hourly paid part-timers I want to. They don't have to be interviewed or even qualified and yet they are the ones who are in the front-line. We don't even appraise our part-timers. We might invite them to staff development days but they never come because we don't pay them for it.' *Head of Management and Accountancy*

Reflection

Quality systems have to involve *everyone* in an organisation to be fully effective. Part-time lecturers in FE play a key, front-line role and yet are frequently marginalised within a college.

Quality surfaced as an important issue in FE at the same time as incorporation, contract disputes and major curriculum changes. Consequently, it appeared to many as yet another externally imposed initiative to add to the heavy workload of already stretched staff in under-funded colleges.

Some of the key concepts relating to quality are discussed below, followed by a brief background to developments in the quality movement.

Total Quality Management

Total Quality Management (TQM) is not meant to be something that is imposed on people in an organisation. It is a philosophy of continuous improvement. The term 'management' is misleading because TQM is about everyone in an organisation taking responsibility for this improvement. TQM is about doing things right first time and every time, rather than checking occasionally to see if or when they have gone wrong.

To embrace TQM is to engage in a culture change which in colleges is difficult to bring about and takes considerable time to implement. It is not simply about changing people's behaviour but also about changing the way in which colleges are managed and led. Systems and procedures need to be supportive and easy to use. Resources and the physical environment also have to be appropriate as they impact on people's ability to work effectively. This is not to suggest that workable procedures or good resources in themselves necessarily result in a high quality service. However, without them, it is much more difficult to work to a high standard. The motivation of all staff, as discussed in Chapter 1, is also important in achieving and maintaining a 'quality service':

Quality certification

Organisations can apply for accreditation of quality standards. The most well known is the British Standard (BS) 5750 (now subsumed into its international equivalent ISO 9000). The philosophy behind BS 5750 and ISO 9000 is that quality should be built into the systems and procedures of an organisation. The setting up of such a quality assurance system puts the emphasis on prevention rather than cure, with quality built into all the activities necessary to produce the goods or services. BS 5750 and ISO 9000 are recognised as symbols of quality in both manufacturing and service industries. Indeed, in some sectors, certification is almost mandatory, as it can be a condition of winning contracts and custom. Accreditation is gained by assessment from an approved certification body. Certification provides only a limited guarantee of quality, as it is concerned primarily with the establishment of effective systems. The process involved in gaining accreditation, however, can help to provide the foundations of a quality culture.

Investors in People

Investors in People (IIP) is considered to be more suitable for colleges. Although some colleges have taken the BS 5750 route, a large number have already achieved IIP status and many more are working towards it. IIP is a standard for human resource development and training. It is administered and assessed locally by the TECs. IIP provides a methodology for developing staff to assist in the achievement of organisational goals. To become recognised as an Investor in People, a college has to have:

- a commitment from the top to develop all staff in line with the college's aims and objectives
- a clearly written institutional plan, identifying a training policy and the relevant resources
- regular reviews of the training of all staff, including action plans for the development of individuals throughout their careers
- an evaluation of the investment in training and development and in the effectiveness of the process.

As with the other kitemarks, Investors in People is not a guarantee of quality. However, it demonstrates that a college is taking steps to improve the effectiveness of its most valuable resource – its staff. It should be noted that IIP is concerned with *all* staff, not just the teaching staff.

The industrial and commercial quality movement

The main 'gurus' of the quality movement are W Edwards Deming, Joseph Juran, Walter Shewhart, Philip Crosby and Tom Peters. Deming's ideas on quality had a significant impact in Japan where they were put into practice from the 1950s onwards. By the mid seventies, Japan was beginning to undermine its American and other Western competitors in a whole range of goods. Only then did Western industrialists begin to take Deming seriously.

Deming[20] argues that competitiveness depends on customer satisfaction. Customer satisfaction is achieved by a combination of responsiveness to the customer's views and needs and also continuous improvement of the product or service. His approach to quality is set out in his 'fourteen points' of management, which are listed below.

1 Create constancy of purpose for improvement of product and service
2 Adopt the new philosophy
3 Cease dependence upon inspection to achieve quality
4 End the practice of awarding business on the basis of price alone. Instead minimise total cost by working with a single supplier
5 Improve constantly and forever every process for planning, production and service
6 Institute training on the job
7 Adopt and institute leadership
8 Drive out fear
9 Break down barriers between staff areas
10 Eliminate slogans, exhortations and targets for the workforce
11 Eliminate numerical quotas for the workforce and numerical goals for management
12 Remove barriers that rob people of pride of workmanship. Eliminate the annual rating or merit system
13 Institute a vigorous programme of education and self-improvement for everyone
14 Put everybody in the company to work to accomplish the transformation

The quality movement in FE

Since incorporation, colleges have been operating in a competitive market. Maintaining financial viability and establishing a high quality service are likely to be the most effective ways of surviving in this environment.

The White Paper *Education and Training for the 21st Century*, which preceded the 1992 Further and Higher Education Act, recognised three levels of quality assurance in further education:

- quality control: the mechanisms within colleges for maintaining and enhancing the quality of provision
- examinations and validation: the responsibility of external bodies such as NCVQ, Edexcel Foundation (formerly BTEC), RSA, City and Guilds, GCE and GCSE boards to guarantee the standards of their qualifications
- external assessment: the independent assessment of the quality of teaching and learning in colleges and of the standards being achieved by students.

Primary responsibility for the first – quality control – rests with colleges. As referenced earlier, many colleges have been proactive and taken on board specific quality models or approaches. It should be noted, however, that a whole range of external agencies make quality requirements of colleges, for example the FEFC (discussed below), the TECs, NCVQ, Higher Education institutions (for franchised provision), The European Social Fund (if appropriate) and the Higher Education Funding Council (HEFC) for courses operating which are funded directly by that body. All these requirements can be harmonised by mapping how the different agencies use similar criteria. This is complex and, with so many diverse demands, there is a danger that colleges become reactive and respond in a piecemeal fashion. The Further Education Unit recommended (1995)[21] that colleges should make quality 'their own'; they should decide what quality means to them and then work towards a customised solution. In deciding on their own definition, colleges need to reflect on the needs of internal and external customers and the wider community; the standards and requirements of external stakeholders and the college's own professional standards and vision of the future.

Example

'The biggest problem we had was knowing how to implement TQM in our environment. We employed a consultant . . . He persuaded us to establish a Quality Council to steer the implementation of TQM and he advised us to take a "step-by-step" approach as opposed to a "big bang" approach so that we would gradually replace "business as usual" practices by TQM ones. He also convinced us of the need for college-based strategic planning, something that the LEA had seen as its province. On reflection, these three decisions and the way we launched TQM was probably right.'
Principal

Reflection

Inspired by the book *Thriving on Chaos* by Tom Peters, the Principal of this college initiated a quality approach in 1991. The first few years were not without mistakes and problems but the college continued to seek to improve quality and is now seeing tangible benefits.

Total quality management, as noted earlier, is a philosophy of continuous improvement. For external agencies, such as the FEFC, though, colleges need not just to *improve* quality but to *prove* quality.

Of the three levels of quality assurance listed earlier, the FEFC have responsibility for the last category, namely external assessment. The two approaches used by the FEFC are firstly quality assessment based on inspection and secondly the use of performance indicators.

The stated prime aim of inspections and other work undertaken by the FEFC inspectorate is to raise standards and improve the quality of the students' experiences in colleges.

Inspection

The framework for the initial four-year cycle of inspections is set out in an FEFC circular entitled *Assessing Achievement*.[22] Following an intensive period of inspection, colleges are given grades on a five-point assessment scale. In a revised framework, emphasis will be on the college and its mission; teaching and learning; students' achievements; the curriculum – content and organisation; support for students; resources; quality assurance; management; and governance.

It may be too early to identify the extent to which the inspection process has improved quality and standards. Many of those who have undergone the inspection process claim that, despite the considerable work involved in the preparation, it was a useful exercise. It gave the necessary impetus to improve systems and it also provided the opportunity to examine classroom practice. Others argue, however, that it is expensive in terms of finance, time and resources and that the process is unfair. Many argue that comparing colleges irrespective of their social context is unfair. These issues are discussed in more detail in Chapter 3, which deals with funding. The views expressed below are from those who have undergone the inspection process in their colleges.

> It was a very valuable experience, although very hard work. It made us focus on all our systems and try and get them right. It's great now that we've got things up and running.

> The amount of documentation required is ridiculous. We must have spent a fortune on photocopying alone.

> To be honest, it was the first time we actually started talking seriously about what goes on in the classroom and how to improve teaching and learning.

> Getting the statistics together was a nightmare but actually extremely useful. We picked up lots of things that we didn't know but we should have known.

> As an inner city college, it doesn't make sense to compare our results to those of an FE college or sixth form college in a leafy suburban or rural area. Over 70% of our students are second language speakers. There was no attempt to assess 'value added'.

> To get 1s and 2s was so motivating for staff. It provided us with a great lift and people felt that their good work had finally been recognised.

This emphasis in FE on inspection goes against the grain of the views expressed by quality experts. As discussed in Chapter 1, in relation to appraisal, most leading writers on the subject argue that it is motivation, expertise and commitment which assure quality, rather than appraisal and inspection.

Deming's third point of the fourteen listed above, for example, is 'cease dependence upon inspection to achieve quality'.

There is, however, a move away from inspection to self-assessment of quality by colleges. This stems from the view that the prime responsibility for maintaining and improving quality rests with each college. Since 1994 colleges have been required to produce a self-assessment report. However, this has been in advance of inspection and not in place of inspection. A new framework for the second four-year cycle of inspection starting in 1997 will place more emphasis on self-assessment, curriculum areas, teaching and learning and quality assurance. There will be less in the way of intense inspection, with the introduction of some form of college accreditation for those colleges who are sufficiently 'mature'.

Self-assessment

Self-assessment requires colleges to be self-critical and analytical and the process should result in the identification of priority areas for action to further enhance quality.

To improve their self-critical approach, the merits of some of the strategies outlined below are under discussion in a number of colleges:

- peer assessment, whereby lecturers observe each other teaching
- twinning sections or departments of approximately the same staff in a two-way benchmarking exercise
- inviting staff and students to comment on different aspects of quality within the college
- setting up quality circles
- listing criteria and asking staff to rate themselves on a scale and to suggest areas for their own improvement
- using this self-assessment as the basis for appraisal, setting appropriate targets for individuals
- emphasising continuous improvement, rather than negative performance.

Performance indicators

As well as inspections, six performance indicators are used for external quality assessment and these indicators are described in Chapter 4 in the section relating to data. They place emphasis on output variables, measuring only what can be measured. In the current political, social and economic climate, it is recognised that the trend in all professions is towards accountability in terms of effectiveness and efficiency within a given resource base.

Performance indicators do not evaluate the quality of the learning experience for students or indicate 'value added', which is extremely difficult to measure. The formative use of this data, however, provides helpful feedback to colleges in order to improve services to learners.

Implementing quality

Although commercial and industrial quality models provide useful guidance, it is not feasible to 'bolt on' quality to current practice or to simply borrow someone else's model. Pockets of excellence exist in most colleges and quality can be developed from this type of existing good practice.

Example

'The Retention Improvement Working Group is exploring where and how retention might be improved. A series of case studies has been put together by the group highlighting strategies used by members of staff who have a consistent record of high retention and achievement rates.' *Head of General Studies*

Reflection

In this case, the aim is to identify successful strategies already in use in order to provide a focus for discussion and action during staff appraisal. The longer term aim is to disseminate and reinforce good practice through appraisal, thereby improving the quality of teaching and learning throughout the college.

The idea of focusing on the customer, which is at the heart of the quality approach, is in line with current educational thinking on the provision of a flexible, student-centred curriculum. Unfortunately, in many cases staff become cynical and resistant when the word 'quality' is used. As noted earlier, they see quality programmes as another device for controlling them and their outputs, rather than as a means to enable them to do their best.

The challenge facing FE managers is to expand provision, ensuring that the service provided is of the highest quality, while working with a diminishing resource base. For that reason – if not for purely educational reasons – it is critical that for each and every learner, time spent learning is productive, enjoyable and of value.

It is important not to lose sight of the fact that value is derived in FE primarily through personal interaction, even with flexible or resource-based delivery of the curriculum. While the learner needs to remain at the centre of the process, it is the staff who make or break that learning environment. They need to be highly skilled, supported, motivated and committed. Other quality factors are important, as illustrated in Figure 10, but they are there to support staff, who in turn focus on the learner.

Poor student retention, which is of great concern in FE, is largely related to the quality of teaching and learning in a college. This is not to underplay the importance of other factors which affect retention, particularly severe financial problems for students, but recent surveys[23] suggest that students withdraw when personal problems are compounded by dissatisfaction with other aspects of the college.

Teaching and promoting learning is what staff in FE expect and want to do. Enabling them to do this extremely well is the most important factor in delivering a high quality service.

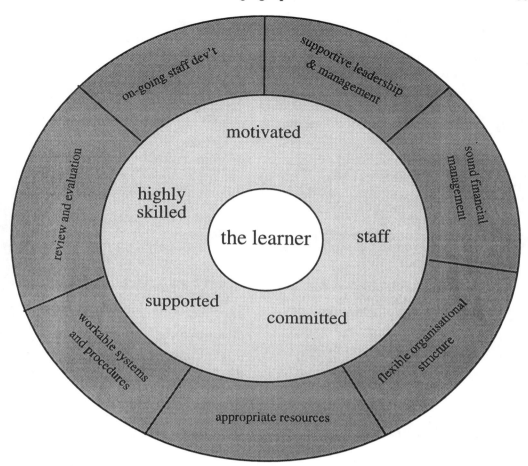

Figure 10 Quality model

CONCLUSION

It is evident to anyone involved in FE that colleges are operating in an environment of enormous and continuous change. Changes on a large scale are part of the everyday landscape and it is unlikely that FE will return to simpler times.

Traditional segmented organisational structures are proving to be inadequate to handle the complexities involved in post-incorporation colleges. Colleges need to be managed differently and this may require making the boundaries between departments and sections more permeable and flexible. To focus on the performance of the whole, rather than simply the sum of the parts, requires a radical cultural shift. Changing people's values and the way in which they operate is difficult. However, many different, but related, factors are contributing to a changing culture, most notably, the pervading market ideology, different conditions of service, new funding arrangements, inspection, appraisal and quality assurance.

To be truly effective, any quality system requires college-wide consensus. Reality must match rhetoric. All staff have to be committed to and capable of responding to customer need. They need to be convinced of the value of 'quality' – for themselves, for the college and most importantly for the learner.

While strategic plans may provide the direction, vision and operational objectives to manage the implementation of change and quality, the factor most likely to be responsible for steering a college off course is resources. The management of resources is the subject of the next chapter.

REFERENCES AND NOTES

[1] Toffler, A (1970) *Future Shock* Pan Books.

[2] Burns, T and Stalker, G (1961) *The Management of Innovation* Tavistock.

[3] Toffler, A (1970) *Future Shock* Pan Books.

[4] Kanter, R M (1983) *Change Masters: Corporate Entrepreneurs at Work* George Allen and Unwin.

[5] Johnson, L and Frohman, A (1989) 'Identifying and closing the gap in the middle of organisations' *Academy and Management Executive* 3: 4–114.

[6] Dopson, S and Stewart, R (1990) 'What is happening to middle management?' *The British Journal of Management* 1: 3–16

[7] Quinn, J (1992) *Intelligent Enterprise: A knowledge and service based paradigm for industry* The Free Press.

[8] Nonaka, I and Takeuchi, H (1995) *The Knowledge Creating Company* Oxford University Press.

[9] Mintzberg, H (1996) 'Ten ideas to rile everyone who cares about management' *Harvard Business Review* July–August.

[10] Senge, P (1990) *The Fifth discipline: The Art and Practice of Learning Organisations* Doubleday Currency.

[11] Flint, C (1994) 'A modest revolution' *in* Weil, S (ed) *Introducing Change from the Top in Universities and Colleges* Kogan Page.

[12] Marsh, D (1992) 'Leadership and its functions in further and higher education' *The Mendip Papers* The Staff College.

[13] Drucker, P (1973) *Task, Responsibilities, Practice* Heinemann.

[14] Bass, B M (1981) *Handbook of Leadership: a Survey of Theory and Research* The Free Press.

[15] Kanter, R M *in* Huczynski, A and Buchanan, D (1985) *Organisational Behaviour* Prentice Hall.

[16] FEDA (1995) *Implementing College Strategic Plans.*

[17] Handy, C (1978) *Gods of Management* Souvenir Press Ltd.

[18] FEFC (1995) *Quality and Standards in Further Education in England, Chief Inspector's Annual Report 94/95.*

[19] Henry, T *in* Sallis and Hingley (1993) *Total Quality Management in Education* Kogan Page.

[20] Deming, W E (1986) *Out of the Crisis* Cambridge University Press.

[21] FEU (1995) *Making Quality Your Own: a discussion paper.*

[22] FEFC (1993) *Assessing Achievement 93/28.*

[23] FEDA (1995) *Implementing College Strategic Plans.*

CHAPTER 3

Managing Resources

INTRODUCTION

On 1 April 1993 colleges assumed responsibility for their own financial affairs. With this responsibility came the need to have in place sophisticated financial systems and associated controls in order to be able to collect and generate a wide range of financial and other information for managers, governors, staff and the FEFC. For most colleges, the management of cash, income and assets was new. Previously they had managed at local level budgets delegated from their local education authority (LEA) and had had some responsibility for managing staff and physical resources. To meet these new demands, most colleges recruited new staff, at management level, with the appropriate skills and experience.

Finance has become a major factor in all aspects of college management. There is now a far sharper focus on the management of budgets, and the decision-making processes involved in how resources are acquired and allocated are under close scrutiny. This chapter, therefore, involves a discussion of finance, budgets and decision-making.

FINANCE

Stories of soaring debt and financial hardship have remained in the headlines of the educational press for several years. The annual deficit incurred by the sector rose from £10 million in 1993–94 to £101 million in 1994–95 and stood at an estimated £119 million in 1995–96[1].

FEFC funding

This situation has arisen primarily as a result of the implementation of the post-incorporation funding system. The funding methodology has a number of explicit aims. It is designed to fund actual rather than planned outcomes. While continuing to reduce unit costs, it is driving colleges to retain students until they achieve a recognised qualification. The system aims to encourage students' achievements, especially in relation to the National Targets for Education and Training (NTETs)[2] and to ensure growth in the FE sector as a whole. The intention is to drive down unit costs at 'expensive' colleges at a more rapid rate in order to bring all colleges to a national level of funding. This process is referred to as 'convergence'. This system is under review and amendments are likely for 1998–99 although the overall philosophy is unlikely to change.

This funding methodology was designed from scratch when the FEFC took over responsibility for funding FE and sixth form colleges from LEAs (local education authorities). In 1992 a government document entitled *Funding Learning* proposed six options and colleges were asked to comment. An overwhelming majority voted for one particular option and this approach was agreed as of April 1993. Specific details, with associated tariffs, became available to colleges in early 1994 and theory was put into practice for the academic year 1994–95.

An overview of the funding methodology is provided below. More detailed information can be obtained from the relevant FEFC publication.[3]

Units

The currency in the system is a unit of activity or simply a unit. College targets are set in units, not in terms of how many students they need to recruit. Units do not translate into the same amount of money for each college. The financial value of a unit depends on a college's 'average level of funding' (ALF) and this varies considerably – from lows of approximately £14 to highs of around £28 with an average in the region of £17. There are a number of reasons for this variation but, to a large extent, it is a reflection of how well or how poorly the LEA had funded its FE prior to incorporation. As noted above, colleges with higher unit costs are being cut more sharply than others to increase the pace of convergence.

Elements

The work which each college undertakes with each student is divided, for funding purposes, into three elements: entry, on-programme and achievement. Each will be discussed in turn.

The *entry* element relates to the work involved in interviewing, recruiting and advising students which is separate from actually teaching them. In most colleges, an enrolment form or learning contract triggers the entry element and this usually earns eight units, or four units for smaller learning programmes. A student on a continuous programme of study can earn entry units only once, so qualifications like A levels or GNVQ Advanced taken over two years cannot generate two sets of entry units.

Most units in colleges are earned through the *on-programme* element, which relates to the teaching and learning part of a course or programme. The FEFC produce an annual document[4] which lists the main qualifications offered by colleges, detailing a tariff for each. The aim is to attach a unit figure to every qualification but, with several thousand on offer, this may take some time.

It should be noted that the unit value given to a listed qualification is independent of time. This has important implications for managers. It is an explicit attempt to provide an incentive for colleges to find ways to deliver programmes more 'cost effectively'. Colleges receive more or less the same funding however long it takes students to gain the qualifications they are aiming for. Some of the practical implications of this are discussed later on in this section.

It is estimated that listed qualifications cover 85% of enrolments[5]. This figure will increase each year, as more programmes are listed and as a result of the fact that colleges can no longer receive funding for non-qualification courses or for those which have college accreditation alone. In the short term, those qualifications which are not individually listed *are* time dependent. Colleges are required to assess the necessary guided learning hours per year and the programmes are then put into one of six load bands, which produce a unit score.

Whatever the unit score – whether it is derived from a listed qualification or not – it is then multiplied by one of five cost weighting factors (1; 1.2; 1.5; 2.0; 2.2). These reflect the differing resource needs of different subject areas. Only very resource-intensive programmes have the highest cost weighting factor, such as animal husbandry, while most business or finance programmes, for example, have a weighting of one.

There are other sorts of on-programme units. If a college provides childcare support for a student, for example, it can apply for certain units in what is called the remission category. Colleges can also claim for the additional direct learning support they provide, for example, for students with learning difficulties. The support relates to specific students and not to courses. Colleges are also compensated if they remit 100% of the tuition fee for certain groups of people on low incomes.

The academic year is divided, for funding purposes, into tri-annual periods. These are 1 August to 31 December; 1 January to 30 April; and 1 May to 31 July. Students who withdraw part way through a programme are funded only for the tri-annual period or periods during which they were on the programme. The census dates for each period are 1 November, 1 February and 15 May. This has had serious implications for colleges, as poor student retention translates directly into financial penalties and this is discussed later on in this section.

The final element is *achievement*, which is earned if students achieve their primary learning goal. Maximum units are gained if the goal contributes to the NTETs, mentioned earlier. Where a student's programme comprises a number of individually listed qualifications (three A levels, for example), colleges can claim achievement units for each one. For other programmes, such as GNVQs, half the achievement units can be claimed where a student has achieved at least half the credits or modules towards the final qualification.

Examples of how units are gained for different students are shown in Figure 11.

Core and margin

A system based entirely on units would not have been possible when the FEFC took over responsibility for funding FE, as it inherited widely varying funding levels. As discussed above, colleges which were funded well above the national average by LEAs in the past are being given time to adjust to the new national levels. Until convergence is complete, and in an attempt to maintain some form of stability, a system known as core and margin remains in place.

The elements of recurrent funding are illustrated in Figure 12. From one year to the next each college is guaranteed 90% of its historic funding in return for 90% of its historic unit score; this is the core. To get back to its starting point in funding and possibly to obtain more, a college must bid for a number of margin units, or additional units, at a price set by the FEFC (£14.50 in 1994–95, £15.70 in 1995–96 and £16.40 in 1996–97). If the total of the applications for additional funds from colleges exceeds the sum available nationally, selection criteria are used to decide

Sue is enrolled on a course leading to the City & Guilds 5850 in carpentry and joinery, a listed qualification.

She gains 8 entry units

potential on-programme	
basic	30.2
childcare supplement	12
total possible on-programme	42.2

This 42.2 is divided into thirds of 14 for each tri-annual period. Sue withdraws after for two periods and so achieves 28 on-programme units out of a potential 42.2. With the 8 entry units, this gives a total of 36 units. She does not gain any achievement units

Yan is enrolled on the first year of a two-year GNVQ Advanced IT course, a listed qualification.

He gains 8 entry units

potential on-programme	
basic	201.6 (168 with a weighting of 1.2)

As the course is run over two years, there are six periods, each worth 33.6 units. Yan gains the first three, giving him 100.8. This, wins the 8 entry units, provides 108.8 units. As it is the first year, there are no achievement units

Claire is in her second year, taking three A levels, each listed at 56 units.

She gains no entry units as this is her second year.

potential on-programme	
basic	168 (56 * 3)

This provides 28 for each period in each year. She passes two out of three A levels and so gains achievement units of 2 * 6.7 (13.4) and not the potential 3 * 6.7 (20.1). This gives a total unit value of 97.4 (84 on-programme plus 13.4 achievement).

Figure 11 Examples of funding

how to allocate the limited finances. For 1996–97, the main criteria are: the extent to which colleges have been successful in meeting their previous year's targets; colleges' contribution to priorities for the year in terms of growth; and the average levels of funding, with preference given to those colleges at the lower level. Quality assessments in terms of inspection grades are not included in the criteria at present but are likely to be linked to funds more directly in the future.

Core and agreed margin are added together and constitute the contract for the following year. As the marginal funding rate is less than most colleges' average level, the system reduces the average level year on year.

Currently, the funding also includes a demand-led element. This element is designed to encourage colleges to expand. The FEFC pays a fixed amount (£6.50 for both 1995–96 and 1996–97) for every funding unit achieved by colleges over and above the agreed minimum units funded by its main allocation. There is no limit to the amount of extra funding a college can earn through this mechanism. Whether or not this element will remain is under debate.

While the values of the marginal unit and the demand-led element are fixed for all colleges, it should be noted that the value of the core unit varies, as discussed above.

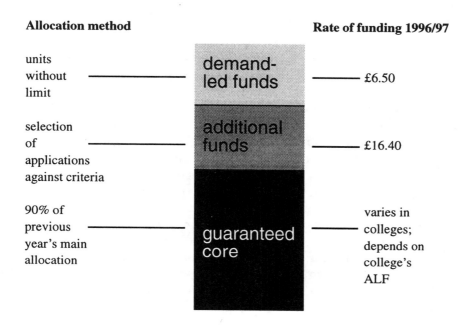

Allocation method

units
without
limit

selection
of
applications
against criteria

90% of
previous
year's main
allocation

Rate of funding 1996/97

demand-led funds — £6.50

additional funds — £16.40

guaranteed core — varies in colleges; depends on college's ALF

Future 12 Elements of recurrent funding

Capital

The allocation for capital equipment funds is made up of two elements. The first is based on the colleges' funded units and takes into account the relative costs of programmes and for each additional unit (£16.40 for 1996–97) there is also an amount for capital funding (£0.28 per unit for 1996–97). The second element is a standard amount allocated to each college (£20,000 in 1995–96) for expenditure on administrative equipment. In relation to minor works, some projects receive 'Hunter'[6] funds as well as the standard payment to all colleges by the FEFC (£50,000 in 1995–96). Funds for capital purposes from the DfEE, via the FEFC, have been steadily decreasing (£159.3 million in 1995–96; £110.3 million in 1996–97; £92.3 million in 1997–98; and £59.3 million in 1998/99[7]). Funds can be allocated as capital grant for direct capital expenditure or as recurrent grant to support college borrowing to finance capital investment. The aim of this approach is to encourage the use of private finance for larger capital projects and the implications of this – and other funding matters – are discussed below.

Implications of the funding methodology

The introduction and implementation of the funding methodology has had a dramatic impact on the working lives of FE managers and lecturers. Some of these implications are discussed below.

The most obvious effect has been the financial hardship referred to at the beginning of this section, with many colleges experiencing huge deficits and redundancies. This had led, in turn, to changes in organisational structures. Managers in almost all colleges are having to focus on how to meet growth targets and yet work with fewer core staff and a diminishing unit of resource.

As noted earlier, the average level of funding varies widely. Most managers in FE recognise that irrational differences in college resourcing are unsatisfactory. They also appreciate that fighting over the allocation of existing resources is not as helpful as campaigning for larger sums to be made available for the whole sector. However, the pace of convergence has caused conflict amongst colleges. Some of the colleges managing on lower average levels of funding feel that they have not been rewarded sufficiently for their efficiency. Such rewards would be at the expense of those with higher levels. Those at the highest end, on the other hand, argue that the pace of convergence is too fast. They claim it is unjust to penalise them so sharply as their unit costs result primarily from historical factors and need, rather than inefficiency. Many 'expensive' colleges, particularly those in inner cities, criticise the funding methodology for not taking into consideration local circumstances. They argue that, given their social context and diverse student mix, it is not feasible for them to provide a quality service at the same cost as a college in a suburban or rural area.

The funding methodology has also resulted in a sharp focus within all colleges on student retention rates. If students leave a course, the funding goes with them. Although this greater interest in keeping students at college until they have successfully gained a qualification has been prompted by financial anxieties, many would argue that this is a very positive development on educational and 'quality' grounds. Colleges should be concerned with the question of why students withdraw from a programme.

Most colleges have investigated the reasons for withdrawals within their own colleges and many are pro-actively taking steps to increase student retention, as the example below demonstrates.

Example

'When we examined our retention rates in detail, we realised that it was much worse on one of our sites. Further probing resulted in a realisation that young students on this site often left because they were bored. Out of classes, there was nothing to do. We decided, therefore, to employ a youth worker on that site, to organise activities. To employ someone – especially a non-teaching post – seemed irresponsible and insensitive to many of the staff, at a time when we were negotiating lecturers' redundancies in some parts of the college. However, with an improvement in students' retention on that site, the youth worker will easily pay for himself.' *Principal*

Reflection

This creative attempt to resolve poor retention aimed to improve the quality of the college experience for students and, at the same time, be cost-effective.

There are clearly both moral and pragmatic reasons to try to address problems relating to poor retention. The diversity of FE means that colleges have different approaches to the provision of support, in the form of counselling, welfare and career advice as well as access funds and crèches. Initial early support and guidance for students are seen to be key factors in student retention. Recent emphasis on a more thorough approach to interviewing students and carefully planned induction programmes have been evident to ensure that students are enrolled on the correct course, at an appropriate level. Three approaches to support services are identified by Page[8]: the first is the caring model, the second is the marketing 'bums on seats' approach, and the third sees student services as part of the learning and achievement process. The latter is the most popular approach in colleges.

It is possible that, in some cases, teaching standards have improved in order to maintain students. Others would argue, however, that the pressure to keep students has resulted in a lowering of standards on internally assessed programmes, with borderline students given the benefit of the doubt in order to maintain higher retention and achievement figures.

The funding mechanism, the move to a more customer-focused culture, quality initiatives and concerns to keep students, have all played a part in providing students with more learning support. The nature and extent of additional learning support varies from college to college but it is usually centred around the communications, numeracy, information technology, English as a second language and support for students with learning difficulties. The support normally takes place on a one-to-one basis in workshops, flexible learning centres or resource-based centres. Although this is clearly a positive step forward, it needs to be managed in such a way as to ensure that it is not just a 'bolt on' activity unrelated to the students' primary programme. The main concern though, expressed at many colleges, is that increasingly this support is not provided as an addition to the students' timetables but is used as an excuse to reduce traditional contact time. The development of learning support is not a cheap or easy option and colleges need to make a strategic decision to invest in the necessary systems and support. A move to a more student-centred approach to learning makes greater demands on colleges and also creates the need for better guidance and support.

Example

'We were providing additional learning support for students long before incorporation. The problem was it was very ad hoc and we couldn't quantify it. In the first FEFC funding year, we lost thousands of pounds because we couldn't claim for it as we didn't have any auditable evidence. Now we have set up systems to monitor and evaluate the support and it is working really well. At least we now feel we are getting paid for it.' *Learning*

Resources Manager

Reflection

In cases like this, the funding mechanism has forced colleges to formalise activities already being undertaken.

The introduction and implementation of the funding methodology has changed the nature of the provision offered at colleges, as many more curriculum initiatives become funding led. The fact that the system has sought to develop a mode-free approach has resulted in more colleges offering students the opportunity to gain qualifications in a shorter timescale. One example is the expansion of one-year, as opposed to two-year, A-level courses. Others include the increase in the number of colleges offering students the opportunity to accredit their prior experience and learning and an expansion in distance learning programmes. When funds cannot be found, however, courses are withdrawn, even if a local need is being met, as illustrated in the example below.

Example

'We ran a really good two-term intensive secretarial course for post-graduates. It gave them just the skills they needed to get an administrative job. These students were not interested in gaining a qualification out of it – they already had a degree. At the end, we gave them our own college certificate. We can't run it like that now, as college accredited courses are no longer funded by the FEFC. We've had to alter the course dramatically to accommodate some kind of qualification. It's not nearly as good and, ironically, retention rates are worse.' *Programme Leader*

Reflection

As this example illustrates, students may wish simply to acquire skills; the focus on obtaining a qualification may actually deter them from attending the course.

This example supports the view[9] that colleges are seeking growth by offering the best funded courses or by franchising to third party providers in outlying areas rather than responding to local needs.

Some colleges argue that, where they have been successfully responding to local employer needs in the past and providing tailor-made programmes at full-cost, they have now been pushed towards FEFC funded courses.

Non-vocational adult education, offered at many FE colleges, has also been a casualty of the new system. Cushman (1996) regrets that 'The contribution that individual acts of learning can make to the social fabric in which people live disappears into the crevices of tariff units.'[10]

Another implication of the funding system is the requirement for managers at all levels in FE to understand budgetary principles and operations and, in most cases, this also involves the need to be computer literate. Those without the requisite skills need to be trained and this is discussed later in the chapter, when addressing the issue of devolved budgets.

Example

'When I took over this job, I was given a budget. I'd never managed a budget before but assumed that it would be fairly simple. I was horrified though when Sarah, the Finance Manager, gave me what appeared to be a very complex spreadsheet. Although I knew a bit about the funding system, there were two problems – understanding the meaning of the data itself and also using the computer. I thought I was fairly computer literate because I use word processing but I'd never used a spreadsheet before. Getting to grips with the budget took ages and gave me lots of sleepless nights!' *Head of Programme Area*

Reflection

In FE, people are often required simply to 'pick up' financial and computing skills. Training is essential if managers are to be effective in their jobs. Lack of appropriate skills can be very expensive for any organisation.

Another implication of the new financing mechanism has been the need for colleges to actively seek out finances from sources other than the FEFC. Some of these are discussed below.

Non-FEFC sources of funding

Not all income derives from the FEFC formula funding, although it constitutes well over half for most colleges. Colleges receive funds from a range of other sources such as:

- tuition fees, including those of students following higher education programmes
- residence and catering operations
- income generation through payments received for courses provided on a cost recovery basis
- restructuring funds from the FEFC to support staffing changes such as early retirements and redundancies
- private finance initiative funding (PFI) to gain access to financing from private industry for specific projects
- the lottery
- European funding
- bank loans
- grants from Training and Enterprise Councils (TECs)
- grants from the Higher Education Funding Council (HEFC) for provision funded directly by that body
- payments from Higher Education institutions in respect of franchised courses.

Some of these main additional sources of funding are discussed below.

Full-cost provision

Many colleges established units or centres offering 'commercial' or 'income generating' courses as far back as the early eighties. This aspect of reaching out to local businesses and attempting to meet their needs demonstrated a high degree of responsiveness and flexibility long before incorporation. The extent to which they generated any significant additional income is questionable but, in many colleges, this type of work was sought after and many lecturers found it highly motivating to work in what they perceived to be 'the real world'.

The setting up of new units to manage and administer programmes, often within the setting of a traditional organisational structure, tended to cause jealousies and friction. In many colleges, these commercially minded lecturers were seen to be occupying the best accommodation in the college, 'usurping' existing links with local businesses and removing full-time staff from their timetable commitments.

Post-incorporation, these units tend to operate as separate companies linked to colleges. Colleges have a variety of pricing policies for commercial courses but in general they either seek to recover direct teaching and material costs or require courses to recover a percentage above the direct costs as a contribution to overheads. In some colleges, pricing is determined at departmental level, with departments retaining the income but meeting the costs from their own budgets.

The lines between commercial and non-commercial work, however, are increasingly blurring as traditional departments become more flexible and provide, for example, work based training in local companies, often leading to NVQ qualifications. This is an example of the ways in which boundaries between organisational segments are becoming more permeable, as discussed in the last chapter.

The Private Finance Initiative (PFI)

As noted earlier in this chapter, government funds for capital projects are diminishing. Attempts by the government to involve the private sector in funding public bodies have had some limited success in FE, despite political uncertainty and concerns. Cost effectiveness and the transfer of all risk from the colleges to the contractor are the driving factors behind PFI. A key principle is that the contractor takes full responsibility for the design as well as the operational phase of the project. Colleges, though, need to ensure that they are getting better value from this approach than from any other funding mechanism. Contractors, of course, expect a good rate of return for their capital investment and for relieving colleges of the commercial risks involved.

Projects funded in this way currently amount to approximately £150 million pounds (and are based in ten colleges)[11]. There are, however, still over five hundred projects awaiting funding to an estimated value of £823 million[12]. The PFI funds are being used for relocations, new sports or teaching blocks and, in one college, to convert a listed building into a centre for clothing design and service industries[13].

The European Social Fund

A key source of income for many colleges is the European Social Fund (ESF) and many impressive and innovative programmes running in colleges are funded through this mechanism.

The European Social Fund was established under the former Treaty of Rome to strengthen the economic and social cohesion of the European Community. Its aim is to help improve employment opportunities in the European Community by providing financial support for the running costs for vocational training schemes and job creation measures. Various initiatives are funded through the ESF, for example ADAPT, which is focused on developing innovative ways of helping those people employed in small and medium enterprises who are under threat of redundancy, or former workers, or employees who have been made redundant.

Many of the projects related to European funding require the involvement of partner colleges in other countries. This, along with the complexities of bidding for any funds, begs certain questions in relation to management competencies and organisational structures and processes, which are discussed below.

Bidding

Bidding is a relatively new phenomenon in FE. Various fund allocations exist, such as the ESF funds described above, and colleges are invited to bid for them. The TECs are frequently the source of government funds earmarked for specific purposes for which colleges bid, often alongside private providers.

As discussed in Chapter 1, managers in FE are becoming multi-skilled. Managing a bidding process is one example of a newly required management competence. Bids usually have to be prepared within tight deadlines, require negotiation with a range of people both within the college and often with other establishments, as well as detailed costings and calculations. The paperwork involved is usually extensive and projects need to be evaluated according to the criteria of the providers, which may differ from the college's usual quality procedures. In many colleges, though, managers are beginning to ask whether or not chasing these funds is worth the considerable effort involved.

Example

'We bid for some money from an educational charity and got it. They provided childcare costs for a certain number of our students. I had to identify appropriate students who met the charity's criteria. I was amazed at how difficult it was to get the necessary information from our MIS. I needed to know which borough each student lived in and their date of birth, as there was an age and location limit. Given the tight deadlines, strict criteria and my inability to get all the information, I ended up allocating some of the money to a student who was not, in fact, eligible and we had to pay it ourselves.' *Student Services Director*

Reflection

Applying for, submitting and monitoring bids is time intensive and also relies on information being easily accessible within the organisation.

Many colleges have debated the value of establishing a separate organisational unit to initiate and co-ordinate bidding for external funds. The extent to which organisational structures help or hinder the implementation of strategic objectives was discussed in the previous chapter. The arguments put forward for discrete units are also valid for a whole range of other cross-college initiatives (for example, work placements, staff development, quality and equal opportunities). Specialist units can be task-focused, as in the kind of task culture[14] described in Chapter 2, whereby people and resources are brought together to facilitate successful task completion. Centralisation, the development of specialist skills and the co-ordination of contacts with partner institutions and funding bodies help to avoid unproductive duplication within colleges, and can also present a coherent and professional corporate image to the external environment.

Despite these advantages, this approach has weaknesses. It can result in excessive centralism and 'empire building' with complex administrative procedures which can act as a constraint on innovation. The establishment of separate units can conflict with the development of a college-wide enterprise culture, as they act as a disincentive to individual members of staff to become involved and, as such, may fail to draw on valuable expertise within the organisation. Lecturing staff often perceive separate units within a college as having a detrimental impact on the quality of learning for existing students, if only in terms of the opportunity cost of providing the new activity. Such perceptions can result in cynicism about the activity, leading to it being marginalised rather than fully integrated into the college.

Reliance on opportunistic funding to meet strategic objectives may be helpful in terms of providing pump-priming but not in terms of long term planning. One-off sources of funds may support the costs of initial start-up phases but often fail to meet the on-going revenue requirements if projects are to continue. In one college, for example, the implementation of modularisation ground to a halt once TEC funding came to an end[15].

Bids are increasingly seen as a way to secure funds for curriculum developments. Traditionally this was funded through 'remission' time from class contact for lecturers but this happens less frequently with lecturers working to new contracts.

There is inevitably pressure to win bids and this is usually achieved by submitting a bid which is lower than those of competitors. Low bids normally reflect unrealistic costing. This may be deliberate on the basis of a 'let's get it first and then worry about how we are going to do it' basis, or it may be that when the budgets were prepared, certain costs were overlooked – such as clerical support, office accommodation or travel costs. Budgets are discussed below.

BUDGETS

A budget is 'a realistic assessment of the resources needed to meet anticipated demand'[16]. This should not, of course, be confused with targets. Budget holders are often set income targets over and above the budget. The reality of the targets set depends, to a large extent, on how the budgeting process is undertaken in a college.

The extent to which budgets are devolved in colleges varies considerably. In many cases, financial crises have resulted in senior managers holding on very tightly to the control of all budgets. There are also, on the other hand, examples in colleges of budgets being devolved down to the level of programme teams.

The approach to budgets is a political and organisational issue rather than a financial one. Seen as a means of power and control, many senior managers cling to the top-down approach; they are still unable to empower their middle managers and trust them to make their own budgetary decisions.

Example

'It's October and I still don't know what my budget is. I get two sums – one for equipment and materials and one for part-time staffing. I've already employed part-time staff, given that our courses started in September. I've no idea if I've overspent.' *Head of Department*

Reflection

Clearly, managers can only use budgets for planning purposes if they are aware of the figure far enough in advance.

Top-down budgeting can be used as a tool to implement strategic decisions. It is possible, for example, to top-slice all operating divisions or starve individual ones in order to fund a new activity or to expand specific areas. Top-slicing and buying back can be used in return for certain developments; incentives and rewards can be paid for meeting targets and top-sliced budgets can also be used for performance managed pay.

Example

'It is college policy to increase the amount of 'flexible' learning. As departments, our budgets provide 80% of traditional class contact hours for each programme or course. We then have to demonstrate that the other 20% is being provided in some non-traditional way, which we negotiate with the Flexible Learning Manager. Once we do that, we get our 20% back. It's quite complex but it means that departmental managers have to go down to the Flexible Learning Centre, find out what they are doing and do something about it in relation to their own department.' *Department Manager*

Reflection

This example demonstrates how budgets can be used to ensure the implementation of strategic objectives.

Top-slicing may also be used in order to build up reserves. There is an argument, though, that this type of defensive contingency funding leads to 'flabby' strategic decision making[17]. This results in the under resourcing of key activities, with senior managers trying to insure themselves against poor decisions.

Bottom-up budgeting requires operational managers to produce realistic forecast budgets based on the resource requirements of their department, section or unit. One danger of this approach is a form of game playing whereby managers are overly optimistic in the knowledge that their proposed budget will be reduced by senior management. On the other hand, if genuine negotiation takes place and managers do not expect to have their budgets cut, they are likely to be too cautious in order to ensure that they meet their objectives. To encourage managers to be more creative in the ways in which they deliver their service, it may be necessary to agree a more demanding budget.

Many managers new to budget holding see it as a form of professional development. Devolved budgeting can enable them to acquire new skills, become more entrepreneurial and, at the same time, be accountable. Support and training are essential, as illustrated in the example below.

Example

'We delegated budgets to section heads. This meant the full budget, including staffing costs, based on the units of activity to be generated by the section. The rationale was to give staff ownership of the funding, warts-and-all. Section heads became very adroit at moving funds from one budget line to another, without recording it. Some also adopted the old LEA model of spending it quickly so that there could be no claw backs in response to failure to achieve the targets on which the original allocation was made. The result of all this was that, as head of the department, I spent more time auditing the section budgets than I had previously spent administering the whole departmental budget.' *Head of Department*

Reflection

If budgets are devolved, there needs to be a clear understanding of the process and the need for monitoring.

While it makes sense to keep within agreed budgets, both over and under spends arise for a variety of reasons. An overspend may be due to financing a new development or it may be related to cash flow management. Usually, budgets are provided in discrete amounts throughout the year, rather than as up-front payments at the start of the year. Managers need to provide cash flow forecasts analysing income and expenditure flow so that any planned expense can be met out of current income. Overspends may also arise if finance for special projects, funded as a result of the type of bids discussed above, are not available until projects have got underway. The cost of paying for staff and other resources then has to be met from alternative sources in the interim. An insufficiently flexible organisation may not be able to accommodate this.

The 'human resource' benefits of devolving budgets are diminished somewhat if budget holders are unable to use their professional discretion as to the allocation of funds.

Example

'We couldn't use ten of the computers for various reasons – mostly due to broken or missing parts, such as mice or keyboards. There was no money left under the relevant budget heading to mend them or to buy replacements. Because of this, we had to split various groups of students and teach the same sessions twice and this must have cost much more in terms of staffing. Apparently, there was still money in the part-time staffing budget.' *IT Support Technician*

Reflection

In this case, the Head of Section was unable to move money from one budget to another, given the very restrictive financial constraints in his college at the time, even though he had demonstrated that the cost of repairing or replacing the equipment was cheaper than the resultant additional staffing cost.

A lack of costing or identification of resource requirements for the implementation of objectives was identified as a weakness in college strategic plans by the Audit Office (1995)[18]. There is often a naïve belief that the marginal cost of any new course or programme is zero because teaching facilities and staff are assumed to be already paid for. This ignores the often substantial costs involved in switching resources and implicitly assumes that existing resources are under-utilised.

Unrealistic costing of developments or projects can have a serious effect on the implementation of objectives and on the quality of service provided.

Example

'We were really pleased when we got our submission for a new course in performing arts through validation. Everyone congratulated us and said what a brilliant course it would be. The submission included a commitment to invest significant sums in the start up cost and to provide us with the accommodation we needed in the new site. However, this was soon forgotten by the start of the next year. Budgets had been cut across the whole college. We were meant to get on with running the course and to recruit students. It was a disaster when we started. We didn't have the rooms or equipment we needed and loads of students left – understandably. To add insult to injury, we were blamed for poor retention!' *Course Manager*

Reflection

Expecting people to manage growth and innovation without adequate support will result in a poorer quality service and disillusioned staff.

DECISION-MAKING

The process of thought and action which leads to a decision is at the heart of management. Managers spend considerable amounts of time choosing between alternative courses of action on the basis of information available to them. Decision-making in relation to resource acquisition and allocation in FE tends to focus on damage limitation strategies due to a lack of resources. However, it is not simply the lack of resources that affect organisational effectiveness. The way in which even limited resources are managed is significant.

The classical theory of decision-making

The rational decision-maker uses the following problem solving methodology:

- identify the problem
- set objectives
- identify alternative solutions
- list and describe possible alternative courses of action
- evaluate the alternatives
- select the solution
- implement the solution
- evaluate the effectiveness of the solution.

This approach assumes that the decision-maker has complete knowledge of all possible courses of action and is fully aware of the consequences of taking every alternative. It also assumes that the benefits for each outcome are known.

Obviously, this is unrealistic for a number of reasons. Possible alternative courses of action may not be known or identifiable. Considerable time and effort is required to research and apply the technique described above, particularly in relation to seeking out alternative courses of action. The time and other resources needed to discover the optimum solution may be so great that the costs involved exceed the benefits derived from the theoretically best outcome. In practice, as discussed in the next chapter, managers rarely possess all the information they need. It may also be possible that the decision-maker lacks the mental capacity to evaluate and compare all the possible solutions.

The behavioural theory of decision-making

A 'bounded rationality' model asserts that sometimes it is more logical to select a convenient and low risk outcome to a problem.

It was Simon[19] (1960) who put forward the idea of 'administrative man' as a more realistic alternative to the 'rational, economic man' of the classical theorists. In the course of decision-making, managers rationalise, weigh up possibilities and evaluate significant amounts of data. However, people have limited information processing capabilities. They cannot possibly take into account all aspects of a complex problem or all the data that is required to solve it. Simon proposed that people do not maximise, they 'satisfice'. Satisficers limit their search for alternative courses of action to those that satisfy some minimum set of requirements. Managers use simple rules of thumb that enable them to overcome whatever problem happens to be at hand. They are satisfied with adequate, as opposed to optimum, returns.

Decision analysis techniques

There are many techniques for evaluating potential solutions to problems and some involve complex computer-based mathematical modelling. They all attempt to attribute values or costs to different courses of action to provide some measure of how to judge one plan against another. The use of specialist approaches – assuming the user is conversant with the technique and, where appropriate, the technology – helps to structure problems, uncover hidden assumptions and to identify where information is lacking. Some of the more widely used techniques, identified by Dixon[20] (1993), are discussed below.

Linear programming is a mathematically based technique used to determine the best combination of limited resources to meet required objectives. It is useful when objectives can be measured and data can be quantified.

Discounted cash flow methods of appraisal are based on the assumption that income received now is worth more than in the future since it can be invested to earn interest in the intervening period. Similarly, costs incurred in the future are given a lower value than costs incurred today.

Marginal or incremental costing emphasises variables rather than constants and averages and compares the additional predicted revenues of each potential course of action with the forecasted costs of each.

Cost-benefit analysis is a more subjective technique. It is used when the benefits and costs are difficult to quantify but are important to the decision-making process. The effectiveness of each alternative is weighted in terms of the extent to which it meets objectives against its potential costs.

Sensitivity analysis can be applied using a standard spreadsheet package. This technique measures the sensitivity of changes, questions the assumptions behind each alternative and establishes the degree of risk taken.

Most middle managers, unless they are accounting or finance specialists, do not use the techniques discussed above. Frequently, though, they are involved in the most critically important aspect of resource allocation in colleges – timetabling.

Timetabling

The scheduling of rooms, lecturers and courses has a direct influence on the quality of the learning experience for students. Timetabling also plays a major role in the management of resources, as the employment of staff and the provision of teaching accommodation represent two of the most significant costs for a college.

Given the number of variables to consider when timetabling, it is not surprising that those responsible satisfice rather than maximise, as discussed earlier in this chapter. Consideration needs to be given to a whole range of factors. In an ideal college, the needs of the students are uppermost when determining schedules; coherent course teams are fully prepared and up-to-date in relation to what they are expected to teach; timetables are made available to students at the time of interview so that arrangements can be made for childcare or part-time work; rooms are fully utilised and appropriately sized; lecturers are timetabled for the contractually correct number of hours with sufficient time allowance for key responsibilities, curriculum development, meetings and staff development.

In practice, reality is somewhat different. The staffing availability rarely matches precisely the curriculum requirements qualitatively or quantitatively. Consequently, students' needs are often compromised to accommodate staffing or rooming constraints. Lecturers are not always prepared for programmes they teach on. Even many of the most customer-focused colleges are unable to give timetabling details when students are interviewed or even enrolled.

Computer-based timetabling packages are extremely useful tools for recording and storing information, producing timetable printouts, highlighting clashes and producing reports in relation to staff or room utilisation. In a truly learner-centred environment, where students can choose from a range of options or modules, individualised timetables can be produced. The packages are also valuable for looking at 'what . . . if?' scenarios, such as 'what happens if we move this part-time group to another day of the week . . .' In this type of case, the resource and cost implications of different patterns of programme provision can be established before a decision is taken to implement a proposed change or new development. The consequences of over or under recruitment in any one area can also be identified in terms of human and physical resource implications.

Timetabling packages can ease the administrative load considerably and they are useful tools to aid decision-making. The computer does not, of course, take the place of the human element involved in timetabling; it cannot solve problems such as a shortage of staff or rooms and nor does it respond to sudden strategic decisions.

Strategic decisions can have a dramatic impact on timetabling at department or section level, as the examples below illustrate.

Example

'We were told that we could not have classes with less than fourteen students and that, wherever possible, we should merge classes. We all knew the reasons why and we worked hard to persuade our staff of the need to do so. We even had staff development sessions on managing large groups. Amazingly, no one looked at the rooming situation. When it came to September, having re-organised all the timetables to accommodate merged classes, we had to split many of them again because there weren't enough large rooms on our site.' *Programme Area Manager*

Reflection

This example illustrates the dangers of strategic decisions which are not fully thought-out in terms of the full implications or costs of the decision.

Decisions to reduce class contact hours, or no longer offer certain programmes, can result in 'negative equity' – departments who have an under-utilisation of staff in relation to the curriculum offer. Without a full skills audit and subsequent retraining, where necessary, the possible redeployment of people to other sections or departments often depends on informal, ad hoc meetings and conversations.

Example

'When the sixteen hour rule was introduced, meaning that students on benefit could only study for sixteen hours per week, we decided to cut all our full-time provision from twenty hours a week to sixteen hours. Suddenly, I had to look for more teaching for eight members of staff. Just as I managed to get on top of that by talking to other departments, I learnt that the new Asylum Seekers' Bill might mean a dramatic decline in the number of students on our ESOL course.' *Director of General Studies*

Reflection

Even if careful planning has taken place, external factors can have an unexpected impact, as this example illustrates.

Traditionally, servicing – the 'buying in' or 'selling' of lecturing staff between departments – has been undertaken on an informal basis and any financial implications have not been considered to be of relevance. However, with devolved budgets and greater concerns about income and expenditure, the issue of servicing can become a source of friction, as illustrated by the example below.

Example

'Servicing in and out is now fully costed and accounted for in our budgets. Mohammed is one of the maths specialists in my section. Since he has been here he has worked mostly for other departments. He has taught maths, numeracy and statistics on leisure and tourism, computing, construction and health care. I now find that these other sections are recruiting their own staff rather than use Mohammed as it is cheaper to employ part-timers. As a result, I am now left with an experienced full-timer with not enough hours on his timetable, while other parts of the college are employing part-time maths lecturers.' *Head of Science*

Reflection

Careful college-wide management of staffing resources is required to avoid this type of situation whereby strongly independent departments, fighting for individual survival, make decisions which have significant ramifications for other sections within the college.

CONCLUSION

Almost all management decisions are considered in the light of current or potential resource implications. The funding methodology has forced colleges to grow while, at the same time, reduce their unit costs. This has had serious implications for staffing, for the curriculum offer and delivery methods. In addition, colleges have been compelled to seek ways to improve students' retention. In response to these developments, curriculum managers are required to broaden their skills and knowledge to encompass financial and budgetary principles and fund raising. To monitor performance and to plan for the future, decision-making processes need to be based on accurate and easily accessible information. The management of information is discussed in the next chapter.

REFERENCES AND NOTES

[1] FEFC (1996) *Annual Report.*

[2] Government White Paper (May 1995) *Forging Ahead.* The NTETs are:

Foundation learning

- By age 19, 85% of young people to achieve five GCSEs at grade C or above, an intermediate GNVQ or NVQ level 2.
- 75% of young people to achieve level 2 competence in communication, numeracy and information technology by age 19; and 35% to achieve level 3 competence in these core skills by age 21.
- By age 21, 60% of young people to achieve two GCE A levels, advanced GNVQ or an NVQ level 3.

Lifetime learning

- 60% of the workforce to be qualified to NVQ level 3, advanced GNVQ or two GCE A level standard
- 30% of the workforce to have a vocational, professional, management or academic qualification at NVQ level 4 or above
- 70% of all organisations employing 200 or more employees, and 35% of those employing 50 or more, to be recognised as Investors in People

[3] FEFC (1996) *How to apply for funding 1997–98.*

[4] *ibid.*

[5] *ibid.*

[6] Money made available as a result of a buildings condition survey of the sector commissioned by the FEFC and undertaken in 1992–3 by a company entitled 'Hunter and Partners'.

[7] Gunn, C (1996) 'Another brick in the wall' *FE Now!* May, Issue 27, Hobsons Publishing plc.

[8] Page, C (1996) 'A problem shared . . .' *FE Now!* May, Issue 27, Hobsons Publishing plc.

[9] Lewisham College (1996) *Equity vs Equality – the impact of convergence on colleges and students.*

[10] Cushman, M (1996) 'Narrow vision of adult learning' *Times Educational Supplement* 6 September 1996.

[11] Natfhe (1996) *The Lecturer* October.

[12] *ibid.*

[13] *ibid.*

[14] Handy, C (1985) *Understanding Organisations* Penguin.

[15] FEDA (1995) *Implementing College Strategic Plans.*

[16] Bryan, K (1996) 'Challenge of managing devolved budgets' *Professional Manager* September.

[17] *ibid.*

[18] The National Audit Office (1995) *Managing to be Independent: Management and Financial Control at Colleges in the Further Education Sector* HMSO.

[19] Simon, H (1960) *Administrative Behaviour* Macmillan.

[20] Dixon, R (1993) *The Management Task* The Institute of Management.

CHAPTER 4

Managing Information

INTRODUCTION

Information is a crucial resource. The effective acquisition and more skilled use of information continue to play an ever increasing role in achieving colleges' strategic objectives. Incorporation, funding, performance indicators, individual students records, quality assurance systems and modular and flexible curriculum initiatives have all created enormous demands in terms of information provision by colleges.

The way in which this information is handled and communicated influences the style and culture within a college. The management issues discussed in earlier chapters, such as employee empowerment, changing cultures, quality initiatives and funding, all have an essential information dimension.

The issue of information is different from that of information technology. Computers are used to store, retrieve and manipulate data and to produce statistical reports but of most importance is the interpretation and use of that data.

The issues relating to information are discussed in this chapter under three key headings: data, technology and communications.

DATA

All areas of activity in the FE sector are under scrutiny with a view to improving efficiency and raising standards. While managers in FE grapple with the whole range of data available, it is worth remembering that, as Handy notes, 'It is easy to lose ourselves in efficiency, to treat that efficiency as an end in itself and not a means to other ends'[1].

The emphasis placed on the recording, collecting and collating of information appears to have assumed extreme proportions. Colleges are accountable ultimately to the tax payer and, in the current political and economic climate, this necessitates the availability of vast amounts of data on the sector. In this way, FE is justified in terms of an infrastructure investment.

As statistics emerge on the performance of over three million students in the FE sector, league table comparisons are made with schools. There are several thousand national statistics on retention rates, courses offered and attended, exam successes and student destinations.

Statistics are also being made available on individual colleges, based on the six performance indicators referred to in the section on 'quality' in Chapter 2.

The six indicators for the period up to 1995–1996 are set out in detail in the FEFC circular *Measuring Achievements 94/31*[2]. Briefly described, they are:

1 *Achievement of funding target – an indicator of college effectiveness* The number of

units earned for the college year (1 Aug to 31 July) as a percentage of the target funding units for that year

2 *Student enrolment trends – an indicator of college responsiveness* The percentage change in enrolments compared with the previous college year

3 *Student continuation – an indicator of programme effectiveness* The percentage of students who, having enrolled on or before 1 November on a learning programme of at least one year's duration, continue to attend in the third tri-annual period of the college year

4 *Learning goals and qualifications – an indicator of student achievements* Achievement is measured in relation both to the number of students and the number of qualification aims

5 *Attainment of NVQs or equivalent – an indicator of contribution to national targets*
   a) the number of people aged 16–19 achieving target 1 (NVQ II or equivalent) in the college year
   b) the number of people aged 16–21 achieving target 2 (NVQ III or equivalent) in the college year
   c) the number of adults achieving lifetime target 3 (NVQ III or equivalent or higher) in the college year

6 *Average level of funding – an indicator of value for money* The ALF is considered to be an essential part in considering value for money

As noted in Chapter 2, these performance indicators measure only what can easily be measured. It is statistically expedient to avoid the complex issue of 'value added' or to take account of a college's social and economic environment. In addition, drop-out rates do not indicate why students leave a course without gaining a qualification. It many cases, there may be valid reasons for withdrawing from a course, as the example below illustrates.

Example

'Six out of fifteen students did not return from the summer to continue with the second year of the BTEC National Diploma in Computing. We had arranged work placements for them all and in these cases the students were all offered jobs by the placement providers. This was a great achievement as far as those students were concerned – and their parents – but we were heavily criticised for such a high drop out rate.' *Course Tutor*

Reflection

Statistically, this did not appear to be a successful course. In fact, two of the students came back to continue their studies on a part-time basis.

The data, therefore, need to be interpreted with care in order to be of value to both external agencies and the colleges themselves. The value of these reports lies in the fact that they can enable colleges and the FEFC to monitor changes in performance at each institution over a period of time. They also allow colleges to broadly assess their own achievements relative to comparable institutions, as well as providing information for the DfEE, TECs, FEFC and the general public as part of the accountability for spending public funds.

While managers in FE seem to be drowning in data, they are still concerned about a lack of *information*. In computer technology, the definition of data is that which is given – raw, unprocessed facts. Data then require editing, analysis, summarising or other processing before being considered as information.

To be of any value, the data needs to provide information which can be used by the sector and by individual colleges to improve the quality of the service offered. The research by Mintzberg[3], referred to in the Introductory Chapter, illustrated the fact that managers often do not base decisions on factual information, even when it is available, preferring instead to rely on hearsay and intuition.

Managing the available data depends, to a large extent, on the performance of a college's management information system, which is discussed below.

TECHNOLOGY

The increased capabilities, speed and availability of computer-based systems have enabled colleges to cope with the vast quantities of information which they need to process and manage to survive.

Most of the demands for information are from external sources. In commercial companies, management information systems are developed to support internal decision-making and are designed, therefore, with managers' information needs in mind. In FE, however, the impetus and design has been externally led, and, as such, the information generated is not perceived as a tool for internal consumption. Information is seen as something someone else wants.

Duplication of data, resulting in different versions of 'information', is a common problem in colleges. This can be avoided if everyone uses – and trusts – an effective management information system (MIS). Use and trust are linked in a vicious circle. If everyone is using the same *one* data set on which to base decisions, more people have a vested interest in keeping that information up-to-date. When this is the case, people will assume the information is reliable and will spend less time creating their own data sets. One data set means that information can more easily be provided to outside organisations. The converse of this is highlighted in the following example.

Example

'I always keep my own record of part-time staffing hours. I get print outs from finance occasionally but I never trust them – they're always wrong.' *Deputy Head of Department*

Reflection

Considerable time is being wasted by both parties in this example in compiling reports and no attempts have been made to establish *why* the reports the Head of Department receives from Finance are different. Decisions are being made on the basis of two data sets.

An effective MIS depends on easy access for all who need it, which in turn depends on a college-wide computer network. Few colleges have the chance to design a new system from scratch. Apart from the cost in financial terms, there are usually 'legacy systems'[4] in place which provide the greatest constraint on what can be done in the future. Rarely can colleges afford to dispose of all computers and replace them with entirely new ones. One result of these legacy systems is the creation of 'islands' of information in different departments or sections, with no 'bridges' to link them.

Example

'We're in the process of talking about college-wide networks but at the moment it's hopeless. If finance send me a spreadsheet file (on a disk in the post, not electronically) I can't even load it on my computer, because I have such an old version of Excel.' *Estates Manager*

Reflection

Problems of compatibility remain and need to be resolved by the implementation of a college wide IT policy.

Too often, discussions relating to information technology policies focus first and foremost on hardware and software. Any policy should, in fact, be based upon the information requirements of the college, commencing with the main issue of ensuring that people have access to the information they need to perform their jobs effectively.

In many instances, information technology is introduced in order to automate existing manual processes. However, IT can provide a range of innovative ways to benefit staff and students and some examples are described below.

In terms of communication, for example, many people in FE are beginning to experience the speed and ease of electronic mail systems. In one college, registers, printed out from the MIS, are scanned in daily once students have signed in. From this, attendance statistics are generated by the MIS, no longer by tutors. In another college, staff create learning materials, publicity documents or reports on their computer and can then send the files electronically to the print centre, which for some people is on another site. Multiple copies, collating and stapling can then be done by the sophisticated copiers in the printing room.

On some courses, students are asked to access learning materials electronically from a network, rather than being given paper based handouts, booklets, front assignment sheets or past examination papers. This means that staff do not have to keep photocopying materials when up-dates are required and students can access them at any time, search for items and print out sections they need. In one, large multi-site college, video conferencing is used for 'virtual' staff meetings, as well as for teaching and learning.

The management of the enrolment process in many colleges has become more IT based in recent years. When students arrive, it is possible to capture the relevant data once, directly on to the computer, and also scan in students' images.

This process enables a college to register students and at the same time create a smart card which can be used as an identity card. In addition, the card can be used to gain access to all facilities in the college such as the library, photocopiers and flexible learning centre, as well as for payment in the refectory or sports centre.

Innovative ways of using information technology are often associated with business process re-engineering (BPR), which was discussed in the Introductory Chapter and also in Chapter 2. It is an idea which has been fashionable since the early nineties and it involves the re-examination of existing processes. As with many new ideas, it has been dismissed by some as simply a 'fad'. Many organisations, however, have claimed considerable success in recent years with their attempts at BPR.

Although BPR is usually discussed in relation to information technology, it is not about introducing new IT systems. Neither is it about automating existing processes. It is, however, concerned with the examination of processes, and new processes often depend on new or different IT systems. This is why it is necessary to have a good grasp of the capabilities and limitations of IT systems, as well as an understanding of the relevant 'business' processes, when involved in re-engineering.

Definitions of BPR usually involve language such as *fundamental, radical* and *dramatic*. It is about a fundamental re-think; a radical re-design of processes to achieve dramatic improvements in an organisation. It requires people to reject conventional wisdom and the assumptions of the past. BPR can be used for small-scale reorganisations (such as recording and paying invoices) to complete institution-wide changes. In their book on the subject, Hammer and Champy[5] suggest that, where it has been successful, the following features are often present:

- work is performed in the most appropriate place
- checks and controls are reduced
- functional departments are no longer appropriate for the process concerned
- specialisation is reduced – people are more likely to be case managers or 'hybrids' and jobs become more varied
- roles change from being controlled to being empowered
- job preparation involves more education and less training
- the focus changes from activity to results.

BPR is a top-down exercise. It requires the commitment of the senior management. It involves examining processes and arriving at simple truths about their purpose and operation. It requires people to have complete freedom to challenge existing processes. It is often painful for some of those involved and it may result in job losses. Consequently, the more cynical describe BPR as a euphemism for making redundancies. As with any other attempt at change, it needs to be explained to the employees concerned, as discussed in Chapter 2. The case has to be presented within the appropriate context. It is important to explain why patching will not work and to identify the cost of inaction. To succeed, it is necessary to have specific quantitative goals for performance improvement, assigned responsibility for achieving these goals, clearly set-out milestones and regular meetings to assess progress.

It is estimated that approximately 70% of BPR attempts fail. This is often due to people settling for minor results or patching rather than re-thinking. Many give up too soon or place constraints on the people concerned. Others attempt to re-engineer from the bottom up or fail because they try to keep everyone happy. Another mistake is to allow vested interests to block success.

However, many attempts *are* successful and they result in dramatic improvements, as illustrated by the following case study.

Managing student retention statistics – a case study

The Assistant Principal, in this case study, needs regular access to the retention figures in order to estimate the extent to which the college is meeting its target units. Figure 13 illustrates the 'old' process before BPR.

The Assistant
Principal receives
regular (out of date)
information

Course leader receives figures and memo. He is frustrated by the fact that the figures are out-of-date as usual. He waits a few days because he needs to chase up some students he is not sure about

The Head of School receives retention figures. She sends each page to the relevant course leader, with a memo, emphasising the importance of editing the print out and returning it to her as soon as possible.

2 days

4 days

6 days

6 days

The Head of School looks at all the figures. She waits until she has collected the figures in from all her team and then sends the update to the MIS section

The MIS clerk keys in the data and sends updated printouts to the Heads of School. He also sends copies to the Assistant Principal

Figure 13 The old process

The old process

The course leader (and he is only one of seventy-three course leaders in the college) is constantly frustrated by requests for up-dates in relation to how many of his students have withdrawn. The printouts he receives are always out-of-date and he sees little point in editing them. They seem to disappear into a 'black hole' somewhere. He feels it is difficult to prioritise this task over other demands on his time.

The Head of School (one of nine in the college) is also frustrated. She never has a clear idea as to how many students are still 'active' in her School. She is pressurised by those above to produce figures and yet she feels anxious about putting more work on to the course leaders. She knows how they feel and how busy they are. She can also understand why they do not see it as a priority.

The MIS clerk keys in data all day. He does not know any of the students concerned and sometimes he cannot read the annotations made by course leaders on the printouts. He does not usually contact them to clarify issues but edits what he can and sends out new up-dates.

The Assistant Principal regularly receives up-dates on retention but is aware that they are out-of-date. He feels that this information is better than none. He recognises that the system is not working as well as it could, but the problem seems too large to tackle and he does not know where to begin.

The whole process usually takes about eighteen working days, by which time, of course, many more students have left and more may have enrolled.

The new process

In the new system, highlighted in Figure 14, the course leader is in control and feels empowered. As soon as he knows a student has joined or withdrawn, he keys in this information into his personal computer. He knows that if the information is out-of-date, he cannot blame anyone else. He is responsible; he has ownership of the process.

The MIS clerk has, in effect, acquired a new job. He spends most of his time providing reports, maintaining the system and supporting users. It is a more challenging and varied role.

The Assistant Principal can now access the information from his own personal computer whenever he needs to.

There are, of course, drawbacks. The four-month period during which the change took place was very difficult for all concerned. In this case, there were no job losses but there was a period of anxiety for many people.

There was a requirement for a sizeable investment in IT hardware and software. In addition, the new system still requires on-going staff training and support.

The benefits of the new system, however, are considerable. Only one person is involved in entering and editing the data for any one course and this reduces the risk of error, particularly as the course leader knows the students concerned. The information is available to others soon after the course leader has keyed it in. There is no eighteen-day time lag.

Four whole stages in the process have been eliminated. The saving in time, effort and frustration is enormous. It must be multiplied by seventy-three for the course

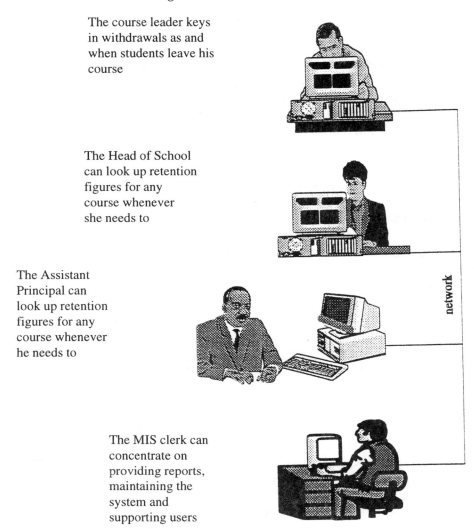

The course leader keys in withdrawals as and when students leave his course

The Head of School can look up retention figures for any course whenever she needs to

The Assistant Principal can look up retention figures for any course whenever he needs to

network

The MIS clerk can concentrate on providing reports, maintaining the system and supporting users

Figure 14 The new process

leader and nine for Head of School in order to appreciate the magnitude of the advantages to the college as a whole. The Head of School has a much better picture of student numbers in her School and can plan accordingly. The Assistant Principal has the vital information he needs, on which to base strategic decisions.

The example certainly fits the description of BPR. The re-think was *fundamental*; the change was *radical* and the improvements were *dramatic*.

Information management involves an understanding of both statistics and computing but of equal, if not greater, importance is the way in which information is communicated within a college.

COMMUNICATION

Communication is an integral part of all the elements of the management process.

A communication system links together the constituent parts of a college and enables the co-ordination of activities. FE managers spend most of their working hours exchanging information – with one another, with teams, subordinates, superiors, students, employers, examining bodies, verifiers etc. They do this in different ways: face-to-face, at meetings, on the telephone, by memoranda or letters or by e-mail. They also send and receive information through notices, reports, minutes and newsletters. Informal communication is as important and this includes ad hoc meetings at the photocopier, over lunch or in the corridor.

The 'grapevine' can be far more effective at transmitting a message than the recognised official channel. The grapevine becomes more active in times of anxiety, particularly when there is a general feeling that important information is being withheld by senior managers or governors. Rumours relating to redundancies or scandals, for example, are rapidly and widely dispersed unofficially. Although it is strictly unofficial, some people hold key positions within the grapevine and become recognised as a source of valuable, up-to-date knowledge.

Example

'Quite often, when I want something known in the department, I'll tell Robin. I know that he'll tell everyone else. For some reason, coming from him it seems to have more authority than it does if it originates from me in some written form!' *Head of School*

Reflection

Those, like Robin, who have status within the grapevine are often used 'unofficially' by others to broadcast information. They recognise it as a fast and effective means of communication.

Information passed along the grapevine, though, often becomes distorted or exaggerated at different stages of transmission and it tends to be overly pessimistic.

Information filtering

The role of middle managers is frequently one of information filterer. Heads of departments, schools or sections are required to pass on information from senior management. They are more likely to be passing information down than up. The taller the hierarchy, the longer it takes for communication to trickle up or down and the greater the probability of the message becoming distorted or lost. In some colleges, the value of horizontal communication is not formally recognised, as illustrated by the example below.

Example

'One of the Programme Area Managers wrote to all the other PAMs and suggested that we ought to meet separately as a group without the senior management team present.

We started occasional, informal lunch time meetings and it was very valuable to freely exchange ideas and compare notes. We wrote to the Principal to tell her that we were meeting, as we did not want anyone to think that it was in any way 'clandestine'. Instead of being pleased that we were using our lunch breaks to talk about our work, she wrote and told us that, as the group did not fit into the formal committee structure, she felt it would be of limited value!' *Programme Area Manager*

Reflection

The focus, in this college, was on vertical communication. As such, opportunities were being lost for people who have the same role, to get together and share experiences.

Interpretation of received information varies constantly depending on individuals' values, position or background. It may also depend on a reference group with whom they associate, for example 'management', 'lecturers', 'technicians', 'NATFHE', a specific religious or ethnic group or even a 'coffee club' as in the example below.

Example

'I consulted with people about rearranging the classrooms and technician area over the summer. I thought they would be pleased about all the new furniture and special cupboards to house students' portfolios. Complaints about lack of storage space for portfolios had been on the minutes of almost all course committee meetings last year. When it came to knocking down walls and rearranging rooms, however, we had to remove a sink in the corner of one room. In doing this, I 'destroyed' an informal 'coffee club'. Rather than go down to the canteen, one particular course team made their coffee or tea around this small area and they all contributed to the costs involved.

I sent a memo explaining the changes. They were furious when they returned from the break. They saw it as a right being removed rather than a new and more appropriate resource being made available for certain groups of students and staff. I made things worse by suggesting that it might be a good idea for them to go down to the canteen and mix with people from other departments.' *Head of School*

Reflection

It was not just a question of making a drink, of course. This group met informally on a daily basis and these meetings provided an important source of group cohesion, communication and information exchange. The Head of School, although trying to respond to her teams' demands, failed to take this important factor into consideration when weighing up all the pros and cons of this refurbishment project.

Effective communication systems

Many people in FE argue that they receive too much information and that they have to empty their full pigeon holes several times a day. Before reading what is in the pile, they are more likely to act upon a telephone call or respond immediately to someone who comes to see them unexpectedly, even though these problems may not be a high priority. The importance of distinguishing between urgent and important was stressed in Chapter 1, in the section on time management. In terms of managing incoming paperwork, it is helpful to deal with a document just once rather than handle it repeatedly. This happens when you read a report, for example, and you try to decide what action to take. You read it, decide not to take any action for the moment and place it in another pile. The same process is then repeated the next day and the document needs reading again to refresh the memory. Time management specialists[6] recommend that one of four actions should be taken with any new document received – act on it, file it, pass it on or bin it. The aim is to avoid postponed decision-making.

In terms of outgoing paperwork, it is helpful to avoid creating lengthy reports, minutes which fail to identify decisions or action and excessive jargon, all of which alienate the recipient rather than convey the message. Some organisations have successfully instituted a 'house rule' that all reports should be restricted to no more than one side of A4. Further detail or background material can be made available by the author to any readers who request it.

In many cases, of course, weighty, complex documentation comes from external agencies but that does not prevent relevant staff reading it and summarising the key points for others. Copying such documents and distributing them can be costly and ineffectual. It may appear to save the sender some time but this is of little value if recipients do not read it.

If clear, accurate and comprehensive information is presented in an open and appropriate manner, people are less likely to rely on the grapevine. Informing people that the minutes of academic board, governors' meetings or senior management team meetings are held in the library – rather than informing them directly of major decisions or developments – is not helpful for the majority of staff.

Example

'Recognising the importance of open communication, we now publish the key decisions made at each SMT meetings in our staff newsletter. We also identify who is responsible for actions agreed.' *Principal*

Reflection

In this college, staff are now more aware of what senior managers do and talk about and where the impetus for certain directions is coming from. Staff can still look at the minutes in the library if they so wish.

Colleges with college-wide computer networks can make key documents such as the strategic plan, staff handbook and policies available to everyone electronically. This has the advantage of avoiding large print runs and the associated problems of distribution. People can assess any of these documents and, if required, print them out. Knowing that these documents are easily accessible is important, even if people choose not to read them.

Managers have ample opportunity to communicate with others. They are in a position to call meetings, use notice boards, send out memos and edit internal newsletters. While some non-managers in colleges may have opportunities to contribute their thoughts and ideas through participation on committees, working parties or a union, many others may feel unable to make suggestions. Some colleges have addressed this issue by providing suggestion boxes, regular sections in the newsletter for people to express their views or even, as in one college, a free lunch in the trainee restaurant for the best 'improvement' suggestions. Another college is running a 'how to make your voice heard' campaign.

Example

'We carried out an employee opinion survey and then one-to-one interviews by a management consultant. The picture was bleak. Staff complained about poor communication, heavy work loads and job insecurity. As a result we restructured the SMT, appointing a Vice Principal for human resource management and communications and four heads of faculty to support the line management functions. These were defined in terms of staff development, mentoring, coaching, communications and providing practical support to the classroom teacher. Communication systems were overhauled, so too were systems for staff participation, particularly through the Academic Board structures and a new suggestion scheme.' *Principal*

Reflection

The improvement of upward communication requires management action, as this example illustrates.

Discussions or informal meetings to facilitate communication between different groups of people within a college can have a dramatic impact, as illustrated in the example below.

Example

'Everyone moans about the MIS. They are always asking us for information, rather than providing it. As part of our educational management course, which we are doing in-house, Ellen came to talk to us about the management information system. It wasn't a formal presentation. She just sat down and talked through what her job was about. She told us why the information was critical in terms of funding and why she needed certain information from us. She also pointed out the importance of deadlines for her section. She has to provide information for all sorts of external agencies and requirements are constantly changing.

We realised that curriculum managers tend to think they are the only ones experiencing change and "hardship". Ellen explained that the MIS section was also under-staffed but she gets little sympathy given the needs for more teaching staff. It was incredibly valuable to see things from her perspective. Now when I see memos from her, I react in a totally different way and I answer as soon as possible!' *Section Manager*

Reflection

This exercise proved to be so useful that similar arrangements are being made for Ellen to talk to small groups across the whole college.

Discussions and meetings can, of course, be very time-consuming and not everyone can attend. Memos are often used to communicate a specific message instead of arranging meetings because they are easy and quick to create, they provide a written record and they can be distributed to everyone. (This does not mean, of course, that everyone reads them.) However, as noted in Chapter 2, in relation to communicating change, a memo or written announcement is not necessarily the best way to inform people about an important change or event. In many cases, the written format is used by managers to avoid having to deal with people's responses.

Example

'The Principal used to send out newsletters on dark green paper. As soon as we saw that colour paper in our tray, we knew it was from him. It was always doom and gloom and most of the information we knew already. There was no opportunity to question or to respond. Rumours about the financial situation and the number of redundancies had spread very quickly.' *Lecturer*

Reflection

In this case, people found little comfort in these information bulletins. The fact that unofficial communication channels were clearly more effective lessened the impact of the newsletter, which simply confirmed what people already knew.

Addressing staff in person provides an opportunity to announce the change and to provide clear and factually correct information. It also provides a forum for questions and answers and encourages people to express their feelings. At a meeting, those presenting the information can listen, as well as talk.

Communication is a two-way process. People who feel they are being listened to are less hostile and resistant to change. In listening, it is important to pay attention to what is said, and what is not said. 'Active listening'[7] involves paying attention, making eye contact, showing interest, listening to the feelings behind the message and confirming and clarifying what you have heard.

Talking and listening take time but the longer term benefits are valuable, as demonstrated in the example below.

Example

'I was asked to set up a unit to manage "enterprise activities." I knew that it would be unpopular with staff. Although I would be offering services, such as marketing, they would see me as taking away their company contacts and using their best staff. I would be generating income for them, but I would also be top-slicing it for my unit. I decided, therefore, to arrange a meeting with each section manager in turn (at their convenience and on their territory) to discuss how it would work in practice and how it could benefit all of us. This was incredibly time-consuming but very valuable. I drew on their ideas and suggestions in setting up the unit. I now have their goodwill and support, which is going to be critical to the success of the unit.' *Enterprise Manager*

Reflection

The Enterprise Manager recognised the importance of communication at the early stages of this development. Listening to the views of section managers was identified as a key factor in gaining their support.

Messages can be conveyed in a whole range of ways and it is important to think about the message being communicated by different management actions. Clear signals can be sent to staff, colleagues and customers, for example, as a result of decisions relating to who has a reserved car parking place or which groups of students use the most sought-after teaching accommodation.

CONCLUSION

In today's 'information society', information is recognised as a powerful resource. The information technology revolution and the changing climate for FE have led to vast amounts of data becoming available. In order to manage the sheer volume, there needs to be an effective communication system in place to ensure that the information managers receive is timely, accurate and appropriate to their needs. While this information is required for decision-making, it is only one part of a college's knowledge base.

Many prominent management theorists, such as Drucker[8], Toffler[9], Quinn[10] and Reich[11], have written about the new 'knowledge society', as noted in the Introductory chapter. Knowledge is not simply about access to information or information technology. It may be explicit, in the form of hard data and facts, but there is also a wealth of tacit knowledge within a college, in the terms of subjective insights, values and emotions. This knowledge needs to be shared and harnessed. As Nonaka and Takeuchi[12] (1995) suggest, 'The organisation cannot create knowledge on its own without the initiative of the individual and the interaction that takes place within the group'. The value of the learning experience for FE students will depend not just on management decisions based on hard data but also on a whole range of knowledge-based intangibles, such as intuition, technological know-how, highly skilled lecturers, curriculum design, an understanding of the learner, personal creativity and innovation.

REFERENCES AND NOTES

[1] Handy, C (1994) *The Empty Raincoat* Hutchinson.

2 FEFC (1994) *Measuring Achievement 94/31.*

3 Mintzberg, H (1973) *The Nature of Managerial Work* Harper and Row.

4 Rolph, P and Bartram, P (1994) *The Information Agenda* Management Books 2000 Ltd.

5 Hammer, M and Champy, J (1993) *Re-engineering The Corporation* Allen and Unwin.

6 Nelson, I (1995) *Time Management for Teachers* Kogan Page.

7 Scott, D and Jaffe, D (1989) *Managing Organisational Change* Kogan Page.

8 Drucker, P (1993) *Post-Capitalist Society* Butterworth Heinemann.

9 Toffler, A (1990) *Powershift: Knowledge, Wealth and Violence at the Edge of the 21st Century* Pan Books.

10 Quinn, J (1992) *Intelligent Enterprise: A Knowledge and Service Based Paradigm for Industry* The Free Press.

11 Reich, R (1991) *The Work of Nations* Alfred Knopf.

12 Nonaka, I and Takeuchi, H (1995) *The Knowledge Creating Company* Oxford University Press.

Index